Building Academic Vocabulary

Lawrence J. Zwier
Michigan State University

MICHIGAN SERIES IN ENGLISH FOR ACADEMIC & PROFESSIONAL PURPOSES

Ann Arbor
THE UNIVERSITY OF MICHIGAN PRESS

Building Academic Vocabulary

This, like everything else, is for Jean, Maryn, and Robbie.

Acknowledgments

Thanks to Tracy Lorenz and Melissa Iqbal for their help in typing the manuscript. Thanks also to Amy Hughes for piloting this material in her writing classes and for providing invaluable feedback. Carolyn Madden and Kelly Sippell deserve special thanks for helping shape this idea in its early stages and for pointing me in the right direction. Kelly wins a prize for patience as well. And speaking of patience: thank you, Jean.

Contents

To the Student xi
To the Teacher xiii

Chapter 1. Including, Making Up 1

consist of, comprise, be composed of, involve, encompass, include, contain, constitute, make up, form, comprehensive, all told, mainstream

Chapter 2. Excluding, Not Being Part Of 22

anomalous, exception, egregious, marginal, keep out, exclude, ban, filter, screen, rogue, outcast, alien

Chapter 3. Equivalence, Similarity 45

equality, parity, parallel, echo, alike, identical, equivalent, just as, likewise, counterpart, clone, image

Chapter 4. Difference, Inequality 66

disparity, inequality, differ, diverge, differentiate, distinguish, discrete, disparate, heterogeneous, diverse, contrast, discrepancy, gap

Chapter 5. Changes, Increases, Decreases 92

alter, modify, transition, transform, redesign, restructure, raise, rise, accelerate, expand, reduce, diminish, contract, decline

Chapter 6. Links, Correlations, Happening Together 121

link, correlation, accompany, go along with, characteristic of, associated with, in conjunction with, to the degree that, imply, infer

Chapter 7. Causes and Effects 145

stem from, be due to, derive from, lead to, yield, generate, render, make, favor, promote, be responsible for, provoke, be blamed for

Chapter 8. Permitting, Making Easier   166

permit, allow, permissive, lenient, consent, approval, exempt,
excuse, facilitate, ease, clear the way for, remove obstacles to

Chapter 9. Stopping, Preventing   189

halt, cease, suspend, restrict, restrain, forbid, deny, prevent,
forestall, hinder, block, deter

Appendixes
Appendix 1. Additional Vocabulary by Chapter   217
Appendix 2. Alphabetical Listing of Additional Vocabulary   220

Answer Key   223

To the Student

Building Academic Vocabulary (BAV) aims to help you go beyond recognizing and understanding academic vocabulary to being able to use it. This book can be used either on your own for self-study or as a textbook in a class. Many of the vocabulary items in *BAV* will look familiar to you. You see them often in your reading. *BAV* takes the time to focus on these key terms. It shows when they are most commonly used, what forms they can take, and what other words and structures are likely to be used with them. The exercises encourage you to make these words part of your productive vocabulary—the set of words you are able to use in your own writing or your own speech.

Each chapter concentrates on a meaning area common in academic writing or spoken reports and gives 10–14 key vocabulary items useful for expressing yourself in that meaning area. For example, academic writers must often discuss changes. Chapter 5, "Changes, Increases, Decreases," presents a core of extremely useful vocabulary for this purpose. A student who masters this compact set of terms will be well prepared to express this meaning in accurate, up-to-date, academically acceptable English.

Besides the key vocabulary, each chapter presents 20–25 additional vocabulary items (which are underlined in the In Context sections). These terms appear in the examples and explanations but are not explained in as much detail as the key vocabulary. They make up a second level of learning. You might find them interesting and valuable for expanding your vocabulary into a number of meaning areas. The key vocabulary forms the main ingredient of your learning from *BAV,* but you can add some optional spice (according to your personal taste) from the additional vocabulary if you like. A chapter-by-chapter list of these additional vocabulary items appears in Appendix 1. A comprehensive list of all the additional vocabulary items from chapters 1–9 can be found in Appendix 2.

The key vocabulary includes many parts of speech (nouns, verbs, etc.), but verbs get by far the most attention. This is partly because accurate verb use is especially difficult for academic writers. Please notice that other, nonverb forms of these vocabulary items are given as "related forms."

At various points throughout each chapter there are sets of consolidation exercises dealing with a small number of the chapter's key vocabulary items. One of these consolidation exercises is a fill-in exercise, which encourages you to remember common word patterns involving the key vocabulary. Another type of consolidation exercise is Rephrasing. This encourages you to get a bit more creative, using the key vocabulary to express an idea.

At the end of each chapter is a short set of comprehensive review exercises, dealing with the vocabulary from throughout the chapter. Two of these exercises per chapter involve the additional vocabulary. Following these exercises are some suggestions for writing projects in which you can use the key vocabulary and a number of the additional vocabulary items.

At the end of this book is an answer key, which you can use to check your own work. This will be especially helpful if you are using *BAV* on your own. *A word of caution:* If you are using *BAV* as a classroom text, look in the answer key ONLY if your teacher recommends doing so.

We hope you enjoy working with *BAV* and polishing your English vocabulary. We also hope *BAV* will become a valuable companion in your development as an articulate, accurate writer and speaker in English.

To the Teacher

This book is for intermediate- to advanced-level nonnative speakers of English who use—or expect to use—English in their work at a college or university. *BAV*'s main aim is to help college-level EAP writers move a core of useful items from their receptive to productive vocabularies. They probably already know what most of these items mean. Now it's time to learn how to use them.

This book was inspired by a need I have felt often during my 15 years as an EAP teacher at universities in the United States, Saudi Arabia, Malaysia, Japan, and Singapore. The strongest impetus came from listening to frustrated EAP writers who were sophisticated readers and had large receptive vocabularies. They knew what they wanted to say and even suspected they knew which words to use, but they couldn't force these familiar words to do the job for them. Often I wished for vocabulary-development materials that targeted productive vocabulary and that took the time to address collocations, usage restrictions, and other vital elements of knowing a word well enough to use it, not just to interpret it.

BAV does take the time to look at the key vocabulary in great detail. The usage clues for an item are very specific: In what contexts is it especially useful? What structures can come before it? What structures can follow it? How formal does the item sound? Are there any times when the student shouldn't use it? How is it different from other items with similar meaning?

Each chapter focuses on 10–14 key vocabulary items within a certain meaning area, for a total of 111 key items. The selection of these items was more art than science. I was not terribly concerned with a key item's score in frequency counts. I was much more interested in a hard-to-define balance of utility and vulnerability to error. I wanted to choose useful words, and I wanted to address some well-known points of confusion. The nine meaning areas in *BAV* have been carefully selected to be useful in the kinds of writing most common in EAP writing classes—general description, description of processes (especially those involving changes), comparison/contrast, and cause/effect. No chapter in *BAV* restricts its focus to a single "mode," but many teachers would find it useful, for example, for their students to work with chapters 3 and 4, "Equivalence, Similarity" and "Difference, Inequality," when a writing task involves comparison and/or contrast.

The key vocabulary items in this book form a general academic vocabulary—a solid base of words and phrases useful to students in nearly any field. We don't deal with the specialized vocabulary of any particular academic discipline; for that, students should depend on their teachers in content-area courses. Items were selected with a view toward general utility and enough breadth to allow for important meaning distinctions within a certain field. **Usage Clues** were written to address common and likely problems. Comments about collocation patterns were validated by, among other sources, reference to corpora, including the Michigan Corpus of Academic Spoken English (MICASE); see <www.hti.umich.edu/m/micase>.

Besides the key vocabulary, each chapter introduces 20–25 additional vocabulary items (underlined in the **In Context** sections). A comprehensive list of all the additional vocabulary items from chapters 1–9 can be found in Appendix 2. These are not necessarily related to the meaning focus of the chapter. Also, they get little explanation—perhaps only a restatement or paraphrasing—so as not to distract students from the key vocabulary. Nevertheless, these can add breadth and can form an interesting and rewarding second level of vocabulary learning.

Consolidation Exercises appear occasionally throughout a chapter. These provide convenient points to stop and solidify what the students have been learning about the previous group(s) of vocabulary. At the end of the chapter there is a set of **Comprehensive Review Exercises;** here, all the vocabulary from the chapter comes into play. At the very end of each chapter comes a set of essay assignments that allow for even wider variation and creativity from the students.

This book can function as a writing text but not a traditional one. There is nothing here about the writing process; there are no readings to react to, and there are no descriptions of essay structure or organization. Many academic-writing students have already had courses that emphasize such things and are ready to approach writing afresh from another angle. *BAV* works with vocabulary explicitly and in depth and then encourages students to practice the precise use of this vocabulary in writing assignments.

BAV can be used either as a supplement to a more general writing text or as a stand-alone text for a lexically focused writing course. A writing teacher working with a more traditional writing text will welcome the vocabulary precision *BAV* encourages. Other teachers who don't usually work with traditional writing texts—who already have ample files of material about process and structure and who know how to find readings for students to react to—may want to use *BAV* alone, as the foundation of a writing course with more than the usual attention to lexis.

A couple of disclaimers are in order. First, except for obvious historical references, the names of persons, companies, groups, and products in this book are fictitious. Any resemblance to real-world entities is coincidental and unintended. Second, I have tried to create realistic-sounding examples from various fields of academic study. However, this book makes no claim of technical accuracy in any field except English usage. Please do not base any kitchen chemistry or amateur diplomacy on what I have written.

We hope you and your students find *BAV* interesting and that you find it easy to teach from. Above all, we hope that, after working with *BAV,* your students will enjoy the pleasure and pride of being able to write or say in English exactly what they mean.

Chapter 1   **Including, Making Up**

This vocabulary may be useful when:
You want to express the relationship between a whole and its parts or between a set and its members.

Key Vocabulary

Group 1	Group 2	Group 3	Group 4
consist of	involve	constitute	comprehensive
comprise	encompass	make up	all told
be composed of	include	form	mainstream
	contain		

✵ Exploring the Vocabulary

Group 1. Verbs with "whole" subject and (usually) a complete list of parts as the object

consist of

Form	Common Related Forms
Verb + preposition	None in this meaning

In Context 1

The <u>nuclear family</u> traditionally consists of a married couple and their children.

In Other Words

In a nuclear family, traditionally, there are a woman and a man (married to each other) and their children.

In Context 2

The researchers described a procedure consisting of several <u>time-consuming</u> steps.

In Other Words

The people doing research told about a process in which there were many steps, each taking a long time.

USAGE CLUES:
- Some common subjects: systems, arrangements, mixtures
- The object must be a list of parts (see In Context 1) or a noun phrase for a group of things (see In Context 2).
- Works well in informal definitions (see In Context 1)
- Does not occur in the passive
- An adverb of degree (*primarily, mostly, entirely, solely, largely*) can come between *consist* and *of* (e.g., "Air consists *primarily* of nitrogen, oxygen, and carbon dioxide"). Such an adverb can allow the object to be only a partial (not complete) list of parts.

comprise

Form	Common Related Forms
Verb (transitive)	None in this meaning

In Context 1

A Standard Metropolitan Statistical Area (SMSA) comprises a large city and surrounding <u>counties</u> within reasonable <u>commuting</u> distance.

In Other Words

A SMSA is made up of a large city and the counties close enough so that people who live there can travel to the city to work. (A county is a governmental unit larger than a city but smaller than a state.)

In Context 2

A new <u>therapy</u>, comprising muscle <u>massage</u> and a <u>cocktail</u> of anti-inflammatory drugs, significantly reduces the pain of <u>arthritis</u>.

In Other Words

A new treatment for arthritis (swelling of joints like knees and elbows) works well. The parts of the treatment include muscle rubbing and a mixture of several drugs that reduce swelling.

USAGE CLUES:
- Common subjects: groups, systems, arrangements, collections, regions
- *BE CAREFUL:* Don't use *comprised of.* It's widely considered wrong in careful speech/writing (even though you may see it in some people's writing).
- *A good general rule:* Use *comprise* only in the active form, not the passive.
- Often appears in the *-ing* form (see In Context 2)

To Help You Remember:

Com- means "with; together," and *-prise* is from Latin/French roots meaning "hold." The whole thing holds the parts together or holds them within itself.

The U.S. comprises 50 states.

be composed of

Form	Common Related Forms
Verb (transitive; far more common in the passive—with *of*—than in the active)	*composition* (noun, uncountable) *composite* (noun, countable) *component* (noun, countable) *component* (adjective, before the noun)

In Context 1

The peptide molecule is composed of at least two amino acids.

In Context 2

The third category is composed of males between the ages of 25 and 40.

In Other Words

At least two amino acids make up each peptide molecule.

In Other Words

In the third group are men between the ages of 25 and 40.

USAGE CLUES:

- In this meaning, use the passive. (The active usually occurs with a *different* meaning: "to create a work of music, art, literature, etc.")
- Works well in writing about statistics to define the membership of groups (see In Context 2)

- Noun forms: The whole thing is a <u>composite</u> (e.g., "the peptide molecule is a composite"). The parts are <u>components</u> (e.g., "the amino acids are the components of the peptide molecule.")

Group 2. Verbs with "whole" subject and some—but not necessarily all—parts as object

involve

Form	Common Related Forms
verb (transitive)	*involvement* (noun, uncountable)

In Context 1

Successful <u>budgeting</u> involves not just <u>accurate</u> numbers but also a realistic knowledge of your needs and <u>tastes</u>.

In Other Words

Successfully planning how to use your money requires you not only to know the correct amounts of your income and expenses but also to be aware of what you need and what you like.

In Context 2

The researchers described a complex <u>protocol</u> involving the <u>meticulous</u> cleaning of equipment and strict controls on <u>access</u> to the laboratory.

In Other Words

The researchers described a complicated procedure that included very careful cleaning and tough limits on who could enter the laboratory.

USAGE CLUES:

- The subject is almost always a process, a system, or an event.
- Works well when you want to make the subject seem complicated or difficult (see In Context 1 and 2)
- Some common objects: steps in a process, tools/instruments, conditions that make a process or an event possible, materials
- Can appear in the passive (e.g., "Many decisions are involved in setting up a Web site"), but the active is better (e.g., "Setting up a Web site involves many decisions"). If a person is the subject of the passive (or the object of the active) the meaning is slightly different.

To Help You Remember:

Comes from a Latin root meaning "wrap up," and it is a relative of the word *envelope*. The whole is like an envelope, which wraps around the parts.

encompass

Form	Common Related Forms
Verb (transitive)	*compass* (noun meaning "reach" or "range of inclusion," countable)

In Context 1

The Animal Rights Coalition (ARC) encompasses several smaller organizations that <u>advocate</u> better treatment of animals.

In Context 2

Today's children live in a <u>digital environment</u>, encompassing everything from electronic "pets" to cell-phone networks.

In Other Words

Within the ARC are many smaller groups that want people to treat animals better.

In Other Words

Children are now surrounded by digital things (using electronic "1" or "0" signals) that range from electronic pets to cellular phone systems.

USAGE CLUES:

- Carries a sense of "reach around and gather together"
- Common subjects: groups, systems, arrangements
- Object will be a list of parts or a noun phrase indicating "many." An object indicating a range—"everything from X to Y"—is common (see In Context 2).
- Works well when the items in the object (the things that are encompassed) are quite different from one another
- By itself, the present participle (*encompassing*) is common but not as a simple adjective. It always appears as a full verbal, with an object (see In Context 2).
- To work as a simple adjective, it is combined with *all* to make *all-encompassing* (meaning "taking in everything"; e.g., "the teacher's all-encompassing intelligence").

To Help You Remember:

Comes from a Spanish word meaning "draw a circle around."
In fact, one tool for drawing circles is called a <u>compass</u>.

include

Form	Common Related Forms
Verb (transitive)	*inclusive* (adjective) *inclusion* (noun, uncountable)

In Context 1

The government's plan includes <u>measures</u> to limit <u>currency</u> <u>trading</u>.

In Other Words

As part of the government's plan, there are steps to control the buying and selling of money from various countries.

In Context 2

The order Lagomorpha includes rabbits, hares, and pikas.

In Other Words

In the category of animals known as Lagomorpha, there are rabbits, hares, and pikas.

USAGE CLUES:

- Some common subjects: categories or groups, ideas, plans, schedules, systems
- The subject is not usually a living thing.
- The object is usually not a complete list of the parts—but can be if the subject is a formal category (see In Context 2).

contain

Form	Common Related Forms
Verb (transitive)	*contents* (noun, always plural) *container* (noun, countable)

In Context 1

Each cell contains two sets of DNA—
one in the <u>nucleus</u> and another in the
mitochondria.

In Other Words

Inside each cell are two groups of DNA—
one in the center of the cell and another in
the mitochondria.

In Context 2

The film contains <u>sexually explicit</u> scenes
that some viewers may find <u>offensive</u>.

In Other Words

Some parts of the film show sexual activity
very clearly. Some people who watch this
film may not like seeing these things.

USAGE CLUES:

The subject of *contain* is something that you can "put other things in" either
literally or metaphorically.

- The subject is often
    a work of art/literature
    a theory or set of ideas
    something with a definite boundary
- The noun *contents* often means "parts of a book." (The uncountable form
  content means "substance of a course, plan, theory, etc."—not really "parts.")

As They Say

> *The whole is greater than the sum of its parts.*

A whole thing has more value or power than you would guess by simply adding up
the values of the parts.

For example:

"None of the 15 stories in this anthology is brilliant, but the cumulative effect of
these tales is stunning. Clearly, the whole is greater than the sum of its parts."

Consolidation Exercises: Groups 1 and 2

1.1. Usage Practice. Fill in each blank with all or part of a key vocabulary item
from groups 1 and 2. For help refer to the "Usage Clues" sections.

1. Getting to the highlands _____ a 12-hour train trip, 3 hours

   of uphill switchbacks in 2 local taxis, and 4 hours of hiking after that.

   [Emphasize the complexity of the steps.]

2. The book was censored because it _____ several strongly

   worded sex scenes.

3. The radiation unit known as the alpha particle _____ two

   protons and two neutrons. [*Note:* This is an informal definition.]

4. The pericarp is _____ of three layers, known as the

   exocarp, mesocarp, and endocarp.

5. The department's research _____ a wide variety of topics,

   including food radiation, genetically altered seeds, and alternative-soil

   techniques.

6. Her book collection _____ mostly of mystery novels and

   travel books.

1.2. Rephrasing. Using *consist of, comprise, be composed of, involve, encompass, include,* or *contain,* rephrase each of the following passages (write it in other words). You may change the form of the item you use to fit the grammar of what you write. Change the words of the original passage as much as necessary but don't change the meaning.

   1. Within the economic stimulus package, there are laws controlling interest rates, rules protecting small businesses, and several tax cuts.

   2. The sections of a modern symphony orchestra are strings, brass, woodwinds, and percussion.

   3. In the survey, one group—people over the age of 60—expressed strong opposition to building new schools.

   4. Several difficult procedures are part of cleaning up an oil spill. Among these are trapping the spill in floating booms, cleaning the shore with detergents or oil-eating bacteria, and wiping oil from birds and other oil-coated animals.

   5. The parts of the fluid delivery system are a pump, a valve, an outlet nozzle, and hoses connecting these parts.

Group 3. Verbs with a complete list of parts as the subject and the whole as the object

constitute

Form	Common Related Forms
Verb (transitive)	*constitution* (noun, uncountable) *constituent* (noun, countable) *constituent* (adjective)

In Context 1

Rabbits, hares, and pikas constitute the order Lagomorpha.

In Other Words

The members of the group of animals called Lagomorpha are rabbits, hares, and pikas.

In Context 2

A large city and the surrounding counties within reasonable commuting distance constitute a Standard Metropolitan Statistical Area (SMSA).

In Other Words

The parts of an SMSA are a large city and the counties close enough to it so people can drive from there into the city to work.

USAGE CLUES:

- Carries a strong sense that the subject gives a *complete* list of parts
- Works well when the parts (the subject) define the whole in an official sense (see In Context 1 and 2)
- The noun *constitution* has many meanings, but the relevant one here means "act/result of making" (e.g., "The constitution of a stable union took several decades").
- *Constituent* as an adjective means "being part of the whole" (e.g., "The GCC's constituent nations shared a cultural tradition"; *constituent nations* are the nations that made up the GCC).

make up

Form	Common Related Forms
Phrasal verb (transitive, separable with pronoun object)	*makeup* (noun, uncountable)

In Context 1

Two violins, a cello, and a bass viol make up the classic <u>string quartet</u>.

In Context 2

Strictly speaking, all countries with Pacific <u>shores</u> make up the so-called Pacific Rim.

In Other Words

The parts of a traditional grouping of four string instruments are two violins, a cello, and a bass viol.

In Other Words

In a totally correct use of the phrase "Pacific Rim," this group should include all countries with land beside the Pacific Ocean.

USAGE CLUES:

- Works well when you want to introduce the name of the whole and define it by naming its parts (see In Context 1)
- The object is usually a noun for a group, a system, an arrangement, or an organization. In this meaning, the verb is separable when the object is a pronoun (*it, this, them,* etc.). Some readers might find it awkward if you put a noun object between *make* and *up.*
    Fully acceptable: All countries with Pacific shores make it up.
    Less acceptable: ??All countries with Pacific shores make the Pacific Rim up.??
- Often occurs in the passive, with the verb followed by an *of* phrase, not a *by* phrase (e.g., "The classic string quartet is made up of two violins, a cello, and a bass viol")
- *BE CAREFUL: Make up* is an extremely common verb with many, many meanings. One meaning that could give you trouble is "say untruthfully that something happened or exists" (e.g., "Jim and his friends made up that meeting to get out of a test"). To avoid confusion in your writing, don't use a human subject with *make up* to mean "be parts of."
- The noun *makeup* is usually preceded by *the,* followed by an *of* phrase (e.g., "The makeup of a classic string quartet is . . .").

form

Form	Common Related Forms
Verb (transitive)	*formation* (noun, countable/uncountable) *formative* (adjective)

In Context 1

Seven <u>opposition</u> parties came together to form the National Revolutionary Front.

In Other Words

Seven political groups that don't agree with the government came together to set up a new group called the National Revolutionary Front.

In Context 2

The pistil, stamen, and anthers form the <u>reproductive system</u> of a flowering plant.

In Other Words

The parts of a flowering plant's system for creating new plants are the pistil, the stamen, and the anthers.

USAGE CLUES:

- Works well when the whole is a shape, a pattern, an arrangement, or an organization
- Like *make up,* is often in the passive. But the passive of *form* is followed by a *by* phrase, not an *of* phrase (e.g., "The reproductive system of a plant is formed by the pistil, stamen, and anthers").

Group 4. Adjectives/Adverbs

comprehensive

Form	Common Related Forms
Adjective	*comprehensively* (adverb)

In Context 1

Doctors performed a comprehensive <u>autopsy</u>, but the cause of death remained a <u>mystery</u>.

In Context 2

Albertson's book offers a comprehensive but rather <u>superficial</u> review of genetic research.

In Other Words

The doctors' examination of the dead body covered all the necessary points, but they still couldn't discover why the person died.

In Other Words

Albertson's book looks at all the important branches of research into genes, but the book's descriptions aren't very deep or detailed.

USAGE CLUES:

- Means "taking in all possible elements, approaches, etc."
- Useful in describing reports, investigations, research, etc.
- Has a positive tone; it's good for something to be "comprehensive."

all told

Form	Common Related Forms
Adverbial, usually a sentence modifier	None

In Context 1

All told, 14 new elements were added to the periodic table as a result of the new research.

In Other Words

If you count up all the elements added to the periodic table as a result of the new research, you get the number 14.

In Context 2

Police confiscated a large number of handguns in the raid—253, all told.

In Other Words

Police took away a large number of handguns—a total of 253—after they raided the place.

USAGE CLUES:

- Common positions in the sentence
    at the beginning
        after a phrase containing a number
- Almost always in the context of a number or some other "quantity" expression
- Means "with everything counted in"

To Help You Remember:

Related to "tell" in the sense of "count" (compare with "bank teller")

mainstream

Form	Common Related Forms
Adjective	*mainstream* (noun, countable but usually singular)
	mainstream (verb, transitive)

In Context 1

After a short time at the fringes of American music, jazz soon became mainstream.

In Context 2

Mainstream physics has been <u>reluctant</u> to accept Nelson's "catastrophe" theories.

In Other Words

For a short time, jazz music was an unusual musical style accepted by only a few people, but soon it became an established and widely accepted style.

In Other Words

The majority of physicists have not wanted to accept Nelson's "catastrophe" theories.

USAGE CLUES:

- Works well in contexts of culture, styles, fashions, or other things that involve "popularity"
- Often modifies a noun for a field of study or interest—chemistry, music, art, politics, etc.
- Usually comes before the noun it refers to. It's rare (but not impossible) after a verb like *be* or *seem.*
- Contrast with terms from chapter 2—especially *marginal,* and *outcast*
- The verb *mainstream* is common in materials about education (e.g., "Foreign students were mainstreamed into normal classes"; this means "The foreign students were not given separate classes but were put in with everyone else").
- The noun *mainstream* is often followed by *of* (e.g., "He did his best writing when he lived outside the mainstream of New York society").

To Help You Remember:

The image is of a river with several channels. One of these (the main stream) is larger/stronger than the rest.

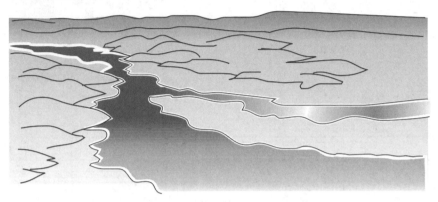

Consolidation Exercises: Groups 3 and 4

1.3. Usage Practice. Fill each blank with a key vocabulary item from groups 3 and 4. There may be several possible answers to some questions.

1. The courts, the police, and the prisons _____ the criminal justice system.

2. Disgusted by rampant crime, local people began to _____ neighborhood watch groups.

3. _____, sixteen fiber-optic trunk lines connected the networked servers.

4. The children of Latin American immigrants _____ 25% of the student body.

5. _____ politicians failed to take seriously the voters' dissatisfaction, so "outsider" candidates did well in the elections.

6. The president promised a(n) _____ reform of the nation's health care system.

1.4. Rephrasing. Using *constitute, make up, form, comprehensive, all told,* or *mainstream,* rephrase each of the following passages (write it in other words). You may change the form of the item you use to fit the grammar of what you write. Change the words of the original passage as much as necessary but don't change the meaning.

1. Most of the people who go to movies on Saturday afternoons are children between the ages of 5 and 14.

2. The university's review of its programs considered all the important issues.

3. If you take into account all the possibilities, there are four ways for our company to increase its sales.

4. In the group of high-speed Internet connections there are the following: cable, fiber-optic phone lines, and wireless digital receivers.

5. The attitude most Americans have about government is that it should be as small and unintrusive as possible.

👁 Comprehensive Review Exercises

1.5. Matching. Next to each item in the left column, write the letter of the best match from the right column. Do not use any letter more than once.

_____ 1. mainstream
_____ 2. be composed of
_____ 3. make up
_____ 4. form
_____ 5. consist of
_____ 6. comprise
_____ 7. involve

a. subject is "whole"; works well if you want to make something seem complicated

b. can be used in the same situations as *form* but unlike *form* this verb doesn't work well to imply a conscious decision

c. an adjective

d. subject is "whole"; comes from Latin/French roots meaning "hold together"

e. subject is "whole"; never occurs in the passive

f. in this meaning is always an irregular passive

g. works well when the object is a shape, a grouping, or an arrangement

1.6. Fitting In. Choose the best word or phrase to complete each sentence. Write it in the blank.

Example: Because of the heavy rain, we had to <u>alter</u> our plans. (mutate, transform, alter)

1. The asteroid belt between Mars and Jupiter _____ the large, spherical asteroid Ceres. (is composed of, involves, includes)

2. Various opponents of the government came together to _____ _____ a new party called the United Front for Justice. (comprise, make up, form)

3. During last year's _____ review of quality control procedures Morrison Pharmaceuticals found several weak points in the system. (comprehensive, encompassing, mainstream)

4. Though its central ideas were accepted early, the theory _____ _____ several other concepts that have only recently attracted support. (consists of, contains, makes up)

5. Serotonin, norepinephrine, and similar compounds _____

_____ the group of chemicals known as neurotransmitters. (comprise,

make up, include)

1.7. Combinations and Collocations. Fill in each blank with a word or phrase that
fits well. Many answers are possible for most items (except items 1–3, which
allow only one possibility each).

1. A DNA molecule consists _____

four nucleotides arranged in pairs along the length of a double helix.

2. A number of communities east and south of the bay, such as Palo Alto and

Milpitas, make _____ the region

known as Silicon Valley.

3. Like most English teachers, Ms. VanTil had a(n) _____

_____ -encompassing knowledge of grammar and usage.

4. _____ involves years of post-

graduate education.

5. _____ contains two hydrogen

atoms and one oxygen atom.

6. Many artists are proud of being unusual and not fitting into mainstream

_____.

7. Lemons, grapefruit, limes, and oranges (and related fruits such as tangerines)

make up _____.

8. A typical _____ comprises two

violins, a cello, and a bass viol.

9. The term *biotech* encompasses _____

_____ electrical nerve stimulation to genetic engineering.

1.8. Short-Answer Writing. Answer the following questions as well as you can in a few sentences.

1. Look at something that shows a pattern—the stars in the sky, the print on a piece of cloth, etc. Use the key vocabulary to express what you see.
2. What kinds of things can *contain* other things?
3. Think about the wealthiest group of people in your country or community. Use key vocabulary items to describe this group.

Additional Vocabulary for Chapter 1

The additional words and phrases that have come up in the In Context examples in chapter 1 can be found in Appendix 1. (They are underlined in the In Context sections.) These terms are not fully explained, but you should be able to understand them from the contexts and brief explanations that are given. Do the exercises below to help solidify your understanding of these words and phrases.

1.9. Additional Vocabulary 1: Meanings. In each blank, write the letter of the meaning from column B that goes best with each vocabulary item in Column A.

Column A

_____ 1. string quartet
_____ 2. digital
_____ 3. autopsy
_____ 4. advocate
_____ 5. reluctant
_____ 6. therapy
_____ 7. tastes
_____ 8. protocol
_____ 9. opposition
_____ 10. commute
_____ 11. nuclear family
_____ 12. currency

Column B

a. traditionally, a wife, a husband, and their children
b. drive from home to work and back
c. a group of four musical instruments including the violin and its relatives
d. a pattern of likes/dislikes
e. being against
f. a medical examination of a dead body
g. involving numbers, usually 1 and 0
h. not very willing to do something
i. the kind of money a country uses
j. a long-term treatment for an illness
k. speak out in favor of
l. a system of steps to follow; a formal procedure

1.10. Additional Vocabulary 2: Fitting into Sentences. Fill each blank with one of the additional vocabulary items from the list below. You may have to change the form of the item to fit the grammar of the sentence. Do not use any item more than once. Some items will not be used at all.

accurate	budget	reproductive system
advocate	commute	superficial
arthritis	meticulous	therapy
autopsy	protocol	time-consuming

1. If our measurements are _____, the levels of carbon monoxide in the downtown area have tripled since 1975.

2. With its tidy appearance, Jackson has a(n) _____ charm, but there is not much depth or sense of community in the town.

3. Because radiation has quick effects on the human _____

   _____ a rise in the number of problem births is an early indicator of a

   radiation leak.

4. People who work in Tokyo think nothing of a 1.5-hour _____

   _____ every morning and again every evening.

5. Only by _____ checking the records for the past

   6 years were we able to find the pattern of mistakes in our data.

6. The dean moved to a first floor office after her _____

   _____ got bad enough to make stair climbing difficult.

7. Putting on protective clothing before medical operations may be inconvenient

   and _____, but it's necessary to prevent the

   spread of serious infections.

8. The senator _____ a health care reform

   program that focused on changing the insurance system.

9. The results of the test are comparable around the world since everyone

   marking the test follows the same _____,

   regardless of location.

10. _____ showed that many of the crash victims

   were still alive when the plane went into the water.

▐▌ **Writing Projects**

1.11. Writing Projects. The following are some suggestions for writing projects that will allow you to use the key vocabulary and some of the additional vocabulary. Each of the topics could be lightly covered in an essay of 500–600 words or more thoroughly in a paper of 1,500–2,000 words. To write information-packed longer papers you should do some research in the library and/or on the Internet.

1. Analysts often try to group the nations of the world according to various schemes—for example, north vs. south, developed vs. developing, First World, Second World, Third World, etc. What do you think would be an effective and accurate system for classifying the nations of the world? Explain your system.
2. What is a family? Whom do you consider *your* family? On what do you base these beliefs? Write an essay about families and how to define them.
3. A modern city is an extremely complex combination of systems for delivering goods and services, transportation, electricity, waste disposal, food supply, etc. Think of a city you know well and describe it in terms of its essential systems. You could approach this topic in many different ways.

    Describing several systems and how they work together
    Describing a single system in great detail
    Comparing the systems in two or more cities
    Describing why some systems work well and others don't

Choose an approach that feels comfortable to you and follow it to produce an essay about the essential infrastructure of a city.

Chapter 2   Excluding, Not Being Part Of

This vocabulary may be useful when:
You want to show exactly how something stands outside a group or a whole. See also chapter 4, "Difference, Inequality."

Key Vocabulary

Group 1	Group 2	Group 3	Group 4
anomalous	keep out	filter	rogue
exception	exclude	screen	outcast
egregious	ban		alien
marginal			

✵ Exploring the Vocabulary

Group 1. Not fitting a rule or pattern

anomalous

Form	Common Related Forms
Adjective	*anomaly* (noun, countable)
	anomalously (adverb)

In Context 1

Although most materials <u>contract</u> as they cool, water is anomalous in that it <u>expands</u> when it freezes.

In Context 2

Grimaldia is an anomalous socialist country in a free-market region.

In Other Words

Most things take up less space as they get cooler, but water doesn't. It takes up more space after it becomes ice.

In Other Words

Grimaldia doesn't fit the pattern of countries near it. The government controls the economy a lot in Grimaldia, but nearby countries tend to let private companies be the strongest influence.

USAGE CLUES:

- Has a neutral tone—not implying anything especially good or bad about the unusual thing
- Often followed by a phrase with *in that, because,* or *by virtue of* to name the characteristic that makes something unusual (see In Context 1)
- The group that something doesn't fit into might be named in a prepositional phrase starting with *in* or *among* (see In Context 2).

exception

Form	Common Related Forms
Noun (countable)	*except* (verb, transitive)
	except (preposition)

In Context 1

Crops failed throughout the Midwest, Delton County being the sole exception.

In Context 2

With the exception of the samples from Lab 4, all the virus <u>cultures</u> showed significant growth after 3 days.

In Other Words

Throughout the Midwest, plants on farms failed to produce. The only place this wasn't true was Delton County.

In Other Words

Almost all the populations of viruses that the scientists were trying to grow did increase a lot after 3 days. The only ones that did not were in Lab 4.

egregious

Form	Common Related Forms
Adjective	*egregiousness* (noun, uncountable) *egregiously* (adverb)

In Context 1

The bank's practices were so egregious that <u>regulators</u> had to take strong <u>punitive</u> action.

In Other Words

The bank's (bad) practices were very obvious, so the people who control banking had to punish the bank very strongly.

In Context 2

The neighborhood's egregious wealth makes it a frequent <u>target</u> of burglars.

In Other Words

It is easy to see that the neighborhood is very wealthy, so thieves often choose that area as a place to break into houses and steal things.

To Help You Remember:

Comes from Latin words meaning "outside the flock or herd." Something egregious is easy to see, like a single animal standing outside the group.

marginal

Form	Common Related Forms
Adjective	*margin* (noun, countable) *marginalize* (verb, transitive)

In Context 1

The true test of a society's <u>character</u> lies in its treatment of marginal groups.

In Other Words

A society's goodness or badness can best be judged by how it treats groups that are unusual in some way.

In Context 2

In the world auto market, the Varva is of only marginal quality, unlikely to <u>appeal</u> to customers internationally.

In Other Words

Among cars sold internationally, the Varva is not very good. It probably won't be very attractive to car buyers outside its home country.

USAGE CLUES:

- Means "just barely in the group; so far to the edge as to be very different from the majority." It always implies that this condition is undesirable.
- Often preceded by *only* (see In Context 2)
- Can imply "discriminated against" (see In Context 1). To strengthen this implication, you can use the verbal adjective *marginalized* instead of *marginal*.

To Help You Remember:

A margin is an edge, as of a sheet of paper. Marginal things are "at the edge."

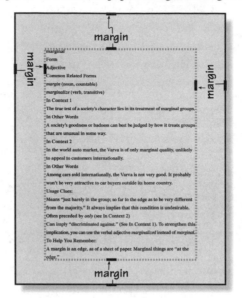

Consolidation Exercises: Group 1

2.1. Collocations. Fill each blank with a word or phrase that goes well with the key vocabulary item. There are several possible answers to items 2, 3, and 4. *Hint:* Look at the Usage Clues and consider some of the additional vocabulary introduced in this section.

1. Virga is an anomalous kind of precipitation _____

   _____, unlike true rain, snow, or sleet, it never reaches the ground.

2. The president won the vote in 49 of the 50 states, Massachusetts being the

   _____ exception.

3. The wounded were in great pain, but drinks of whiskey provided some marginal

   _____.

4. His egregious _____ attracted the attention of the

   police.

2.2. Rephrasing. Using *anomalous, exception, egregious,* or *marginal,* rephrase each of the following passages (write it in other words). You may change the form of the item you use to fit the grammar of what you write. Change the words of the original passage as much as necessary but don't change the meaning.

1. Because she dressed differently than the other girls and spent more time studying, Sarah did not have a very solid position in the social group at the school.

2. Venezuela and Mexico are unusual among the members of OPEC because they have Spanish-speaking, mostly Christian populations.

3. It was very easy for the people to see that the government was spending huge amounts of money on projects that enriched the prime minister's friends. This made the public angry.

4. Most kinds of pine trees grow best in cool or dry climates, but the Cuban pine does well in warm moist conditions.

Group 2. Verbs for preventing inclusion

keep out

Form	Common Related Forms
Verb (transitive/intransitive)	None

In Context 1

Australia's <u>strict</u> <u>quarantine</u> rules aim mostly to keep out diseases of cattle and sheep.

In Context 2

Most members of the marketing department kept out of the <u>battle</u> between the two top managers.

In Other Words

Australia has very strong rules against bringing plants or animals into the country. The main purpose of these rules is to make sure that illnesses of cattle and sheep don't get into the country.

In Other Words

Most of the people in the marketing department did not support one side or another in the struggle between the two top managers.

USAGE CLUES:

- Often followed by an *of* phrase to name the group that something is not part of
- For the transitive form (see In Context 1)

    Common subjects: rules or laws, conditions, characteristics, persons or groups

    In general, an object that is a long noun phrase will probably come after *out* (see In Context 1).

    If the object is shorter it will probably come between *keep* and *out* (e.g., "Discriminatory admission policies at the college kept ethnic minorities out").

    If there is an *of* phrase after *keep out,* any object, even if it is long, should come between *keep* and *out* (e.g., "Lack of experience kept most rural students from the central valley out of the competition for high-tech jobs").

    Works well in contexts of anger or disagreement, because the tone is less neutral than that of *exclude*

- For the intransitive form (see In Context 2)

    Involves a *decision* to stay away. The subject of the intransitive is usually a person, an animal, or an organization—something that can make decisions.

exclude

Form	Common Related Forms
Verb (transitive)	*exclusion* (noun, uncountable) *exclusive* (adjective) *exclusively* (adverb) *exclusivity* (noun) *excludable* (adjective)

In Context 1

In the 1950s, the club excluded people on the basis of color and national origin.

In Other Words

The club would not let people of some races or nationalities in.

In Context 2

The people who took this <u>poll</u> excluded any responses that were <u>illegible</u> or incomplete.

In Other Words

The people who took this poll (a measure of public opinion) did not include any answers that were hard to read or were not complete.

USAGE CLUES:

- *Exclude* and its related forms are very common and can be used in almost any context.
- The subject will always be a group or an organization, a member of the group, or a rule imposed by the group.
- When the object is a person or group of people, the context might imply that the subject is treating the object badly (see In Context 1).
- *Exclusive* is most often used to describe something that is hard to get into but desirable (e.g., "an exclusive neighborhood").
- *Exclusion* is common in accounting, especially in relation to taxes.
- The present participle often appears in a sentence modifier (e.g., "Excluding housing prices, inflation has been low" means "If we exclude housing prices from our calculations, inflation has been low").
- Works well in statistical contexts to talk about a number or group that is not part of the data (see In Context 2)

 To Help You Remember:

- Contrasts with "include" (see chap. 1)
- Comes from Latin words meaning "close out." Excluding is like closing a door to keep someone/something out.

As They Say

the exception that proves the rule

The thing that does not fit in and, by being different, shows what the general pattern is.

For example:

Charles's sense of humor is unusual among the Stewart family, the exception that proves the rule.

This means that Charles's sense of humor, by being unusual, shows how humorless the other Stewarts are.

ban

Form	Common Related Forms
Verb (transitive)	*ban* (noun, countable)

In Context 1

Police banned journalists from the area while they searched for <u>survivors</u> of the crash.

In Context 2

In an attempt to stop the <u>spread</u> of apple blight, the importation of all foreign fruit was banned.

In Other Words

The police announced that journalists would not be let into the area during the search for people still alive after the crash.

In Other Words

To keep the apple blight from traveling further, the government said that foreign fruit could not be brought into the country.

USAGE CLUES:

- The base meaning is "to officially announce that something is not allowed."
- Usual subjects are nouns for authorities (*police, government,* etc.) or rules.
- Often followed by *from* (see In Context 1)
- Often appears in the passive (see In Context 2)
- You can ban a person from
    a place or an organization
    an action, an event, or a process
- The noun form *ban* is often the object of verbs like *impose* or *declare* (e.g., "The government imposed a ban on the importation of foreign fruit").
- The noun is also often followed by a phrase beginning with *on* (e.g., "a ban on the importation of foreign fruit").

Group 3. Keeping some things out while letting others through

filter

Form	Common Related Forms
Verb (transitive)	*filter* (noun, countable) *filtering* (noun for process, general use) *filtration* (noun for process, technical)

In Context 1

The lens <u>coating</u> filtered out most frequencies of light.

In Other Words

The material on the surface kept most frequencies of light from passing through the lens (a piece of glass that changes the direction of the light). (Frequency of light = light with a certain wavelength.)

In Context 2

Official student groups on campus filter most forms of expression, so that only very <u>bland</u> statements are ever made publicly.

In Other Words

Student groups keep most things from being said at the college. Only very uninteresting things can be said openly.

USAGE CLUES:

- If *filter* is NOT followed by *out*, the object must be a fluid or something else that is considered "like a fluid" (light, sound, ideas, writing/speech, or even people or things that move in groups) (see In Context 2).
- In most such cases, the use of *filter* is metaphorical. The thing being filtered is not really a fluid, but it seems like a fluid in some way.
- If *filter* is followed by *out*, the object will be an unwanted thing that is being removed from the "fluidlike" thing (see In Context 1).
- The transitive verb can be followed by *through* (e.g., "The administration filtered all our memos through a censorship committee"). *BE CAREFUL:* There is also an intransitive verb *filter through* with a different meaning (e.g., "The crowd filtered through the gate" means "The crowd passed through the gate slowly and not all at once").

To Help You Remember:

The base meaning is "to clean a fluid by passing it through a material that removes unwanted things." Some things that are filtered: coffee, water, air, smoke, etc.

screen

Form	Common Related Forms
Verb (transitive)	*screening* (noun for process, uncountable) *screening* (noun meaning "occasions when one screens," countable) *screen* (noun meaning "instrument used in keeping some things out," countable)

In Context 1

The hospital screened its blood supply for HIV.

In Other Words

The hospital did tests on the blood it kept. The tests were to find evidence of HIV (the virus that can lead to AIDS).

In Context 2

After carefully screening thirty-five <u>applicants</u>, the committee <u>short-listed</u> three.

In Other Words

After carefully examining thirty-five people who applied for the job (and looking for possible problems that might make them unsuitable), the committee selected three top possible choices.

USAGE CLUES:

- Works well in describing safety measures or careful investigations
- The subject is often a person or group with authority to select someone or something.
- *If the verb is NOT followed by* out

  The object will be the group or collection that is being examined.

  The object might be followed by a *for* phrase that names the undesirable thing to be kept out (see In Context 1).
- *If the verb is followed by* out, the object will be the undesirable thing to be removed.

 To Help You Remember:

Like *filter*, *screen* has a base meaning of "remove unwanted things from a fluid." A screen is rougher than a filter, with much larger holes. Screens are often put on windows so air can enter but insects can't.

Consolidation Exercises: Groups 2 and 3

2.3. Meanings and Connections. Next to each description, write *keep out, exclude, ban, filter,* or *screen*—whichever best matches the description. Some of these items may be used more than once. Some may not be used at all.

_____ 1. means "not let through"; used with fluids or ideas

_____ 2. means "not let through"; can be used with solids

_____ 3. comes from a Latin root meaning "close out"

2.4. Collocations. Fill each blank with a word or phrase that goes well with the key vocabulary item. There is more than one possible answer to item 3. *Hint:* Look at the Usage Clues and consider some of the additional vocabulary introduced in this section.

1. Before the melted plastic was remolded, impurities were filtered _____

   _____ of it.

2. Not many foreign ideas filtered _____ the official

   censorship system.

3. Official policy welcomed women to the army, but many older officers were in

   favor of keeping _____ out.

4. The ban _____ all car and bus traffic downtown

   went into effect.

2.5. Rephrasing. Using *keep out, exclude, ban, filter,* or *screen,* rephrase each of the following passages (write it in other words). You may change the form of the item you use to fit the grammar of what you write. Change the words of the original passage as much as necessary but don't change the meaning.

1. Because of the high cost of tuition at Barstoke University, few middle-class students could attend.

2. Airlines use psychological tests to make sure that unstable people don't become pilots of commercial aircraft.

3. The military authorities would not let journalists into the battle zone.

4. The government had anti-American feelings, so American companies were not able to get into the country to do business.

5. High air pressure inside the building makes it impossible for the dusty outside air to flow in.

Group 4. Terms for outsiders

rogue

Form	Common Related Forms
Adjective	*rogue* (noun, countable) No others in this meaning; some related forms (*roguery, roguish, roguishness,* etc.) exist, but they emphasize "mischief," "badness," or "criminality," not "being outside the group."

In Context

The tumors originate with rogue cells that suddenly begin producing wildly.

In Other Words

The unnatural growths in the body start out as cells that behave unusually—by reproducing in a fast, uncontrolled way.

In Context

Many of the bank's losses stemmed from the activities of a rogue officer in the corporate loan section.

In Other Words

Much of the money lost by the bank was because of things done by a person in the office that lends money to businesses. He or she acted alone and in a way outside normal procedures.

USAGE CLUES:

- Means "following one's own course, which is different from the course pursued by the group"
- Implies bad behavior in the one called a "rogue"—although it can be used humorously, to tease
- Formerly used mostly for elephants (to refer to an elephant that traveled alone, not with a herd) or for people who behaved dishonestly
- Recently common for nations (*rogue nation, rogue state*) that are seen to break away from the course pursued by most others or to financial workers (*rogue trader, rogue banker*) who pursue high-risk ventures without approval from their bosses

outcast

Form	Common Related Forms
Noun (countable)	None, but there is a connection to the verb *cast out*.

In Context 1

Among her baseball-loving colleagues, Dr. Prakash, a cricket fan, felt like an outcast.

In Other Words

Most other people with whom Dr. Prakash worked were interested in baseball. Because she liked cricket, she felt like she was outside the group.

In Context 2

The cult attracted social outcasts and misfits.

In Other Words

The small, unusual religious group drew in misfits (people who didn't fit well into society) and people who had not been accepted into mainstream society.

USAGE CLUES:

- An outcast is almost always a person.
- You can use *outcast* for someone you feel positively about or feel sorry for.
- Some adjectives that commonly appear with *outcast: social, complete, miserable*

alien

Form	Common Related Forms
Adjective	*alien* (noun, countable) *alienate* (verb, transitive) *alienation* (noun, uncountable) *inalienable* (adjective)

In Context 1

The concept of a free <u>press</u> was alien to the region.

In Context 2

Branson claims the government is covering up <u>evidence</u> that aliens have visited Earth.

In Other Words

The idea that news media should be free to report on almost all issues was strange and foreign in this area.

In Other Words

Branson says the government is trying to hide facts that show our planet has been visited by beings from other planets.

USAGE CLUES:

- Most often used to describe something/someone
    from beyond Earth
    from other societies or cultures
- Sometimes followed by *to* (see In Context 1)
- Nouns that commonly appear with *alien: concept, idea, system*
- The noun *alienation* implies "feelings of being lost and confused (and perhaps angry) because of being outside the group."
- The verb *alienate* (meaning "make someone feel or be outside the group") is often followed by a *from* phrase that names the group from which someone is excluded.
- The object of *alienate* is almost always a person or group of persons.
- The U.S. Declaration of Independence includes the term *inalienable rights*—rights that can't be taken away.

Consolidation Exercises: Group 4

2.6. Collocations. Fill in each blank with a word or phrase that goes well with the key term (or a related form). *Hint:* Look at the Usage Clues and consider some of the additional vocabulary introduced in this section.

1. The United States arrogantly considers a country a "rogue _____

    _____" if the country acts independently, instead of taking orders from

    Washington.

2. After selling illegal copies of CDs, the company tried to defend itself by saying

    that the idea of intellectual property rights was alien _____

    _____ their country's culture.

3. Wellington's controversial writings made her a(n) _____

_____ outcast, rarely seen with other members of Chicago's literary

community.

4. Buckman was alienated _____ the Republican

Party by the party's refusal to endorse his conservative views.

2.7. Rephrasing. Using *rogue, outcast,* or *alien,* rephrase each of the following statements (write it in other words). You may change the form of the item you use to fit the grammar of what you write. Change the words of the original passage as much as necessary but don't change the meaning.

1. There is still no evidence that even microscopic life-forms from other planets have ever come to Earth.

2. DeBoer liked to portray himself as having been rejected by society, but he was actually quite popular, and his paintings sold well during his lifetime.

3. The research showed that the cells were damaged by proteins that did not behave in the usual way.

4. Many of the beliefs held by Western animal-rights activists seem strange and foreign to people from poorer, more rural societies.

👁 Comprehensive Review Exercises

2.8. Meanings and Connections. Next to each item in the left column, write the letter of the best meaning/description from the right column. Do not use any letter more than once.

____	1. alien	a. refers to someone rejected by society
____	2. anomalous	b. This word is also the name of a window covering that
____	3. ban	keeps insects out.
____	4. egregious	c. going one's own way; not behaving like the rest of the
____	5. exception	group
____	6. exclude	d. "close out"
____	7. filter	e. strange and easily noticed
____	8. marginal	f. just barely inside the group
____	9. outcast	g. an officially announced program to not allow something in
____	10. rogue	h. foreign
____	11. screen	i. a noun often followed by a *to* or *among* phrase
		j. used in the context of fluids or fluidlike things
		k. an adjective that might be followed by a phrase with *because, in that,* or *by virtue of*

2.9. Fitting In. Choose the best word or phrase to complete each sentence. Write it in the blank.

> *Example:* Because of the heavy rain, we had to <u>alter</u> our plans. (mutate, transform, alter)

1. Worried that competitors might try to steal business secrets, Montnova, Inc., carefully _____ all visitors to its offices. (screened, filtered, excluded)

2. There's an _____ to every rule. (alien, exclusion, exception)

3. The president's efforts to improve his image were only _____ _____ successful. (marginally, egregiously, exclusively)

4. Much of the unpleasant truth about the situation was _____ _____ out by the sales force before reaching the management. (banned, alienated, filtered)

5. Europe's _____ on British beef caused a lot of ill

   feeling in the U.K. (exclusion, ban, filter)

6. Basketball is _____ among American team sports

   in that it has attracted a lot of fans internationally. (rogue, egregious, anomalous)

7. If you _____ rises in the price of oil, the cost of

   living has risen only about 2 percent this year. (exclude, filter out, ban)

2.10. Matching. Match each item in the left column with a word from the right
      column.

1. a rogue _____   concept

2. an alien _____   rule

3. a _____ outcast   behavior

4. a ban on _____   trader

5. an exception to the _____   imports

6. egregious _____   social

2.11. Combinations and Collocations. Fill in each blank with a word or phrase
      that fits well with the key vocabulary item. Many answers are possible for
      items 2–8.

1. Our program of counseling aims to relieve the sense of alienation _____

   _____ their parents that many teenagers

   feel.

2. Trading losses by a rogue _____

   _____ named Chip Freedman nearly ruined the securities firm of Jones and

   Whitcomb, Inc.

3. Ostriches are anomalous in that _____

   _____ .

4. Once extremely rich, the tennis star Lenny Brown was driven to poverty by his

   egregious _____ .

5. U.S. tax authorities do not allow deductions for the interest on most debt, but

   they _____ an exception for

   the interest on home mortgages.

6. The first step in measuring pollution in a given volume of air is to filter out

   _____ and weigh it.

7. When speaking about North America, many people exclude _____

   _____.

8. In interviewing people for jobs involving the handling of money, it's important

   to screen for _____.

Additional Vocabulary for Chapter 2

The additional words that have come up in the In Context examples in chapter 2 can be found in Appendix 1. (They are underlined when they occur in the In Context sections.) These terms are not fully explained, but you should be able to understand them from the contexts and brief explanations that are given. Do the exercises below to help solidify your understanding of these words.

2.12. Additional Vocabulary 1: Meanings. In each blank, write the letter of the meaning from column B that goes best with each vocabulary item in column A.

Column A
____ 1. regulator
____ 2. punitive
____ 3. misfit
____ 4. poll
____ 5. applicant
____ 6. contract
____ 7. expand
____ 8. culture
____ 9. press
____ 10. character
____ 11. target
____ 12. loan

Column B
a. a sample of an organism being grown for research purposes
b. someone who has asked for a job or position
c. a measure of public opinion
d. something that people shoot at
e. someone who sets the rules that control an activity
f. newspapers, magazines, radio, etc.
g. personality; the way you are
h. money you may use but that you must pay back
i. get bigger
j. get smaller
k. someone who doesn't easily fit into a group
l. related to punishment

2.13. Additional Vocabulary 2: Fitting into Sentences. Fill each blank with one of the additional vocabulary items from the list below. Do not use any item more than once. Some items will not be used at all.

appeal	originate	strict
bland	quarantine	survivor
contract	regulator	tumor
evidence	short-list	
expand	spread	

1. We used _____ quality-control procedures to make sure the equipment would work as it should.

2. The food on airplanes is always too _____ for me, so I put some hot sauce on it to make it more interesting.

3. About 20 companies submitted proposals. In the end, the agency _____

    _____ 4 of them for further consideration.

4. Roads in Minnesota crack very easily because the pavement _____

    _____ a lot in the hot summer and then _____ in the

    severe winter cold.

5. There was a lot of _____ indicating that the president's

    friends had stolen millions of dollars of public money, but none of these

    powerful figures was ever brought to court.

6. People who have regained their health after fighting cancer think of themselves

    as _____ , as if they had lived through a catastrophe like

    an earthquake or a car crash.

7. The economic crisis _____ in East Asia and then

    _____ throughout the world.

8. Brightly colored furniture doesn't _____ to me. Softer

    earth tones like brown or gray are more in line with my tastes.

🎬 Writing Projects

2.14. Writing Projects. The following are some suggestions for writing projects that will allow you to use the key vocabulary and some of the additional vocabulary. Each of the topics could be lightly covered in an essay of 500–600 words or more thoroughly in a paper of 1,500–2,000 words. To write information-packed longer papers you should do some research in the library and/or on the Internet.

1. Many countries are worried about the spread of potentially deadly diseases—such as tuberculosis, AIDS, hepatitis, or various other illnesses—that don't respond well to treatment. However, it is not practical for any country to totally shut itself away from others. Trade must go on. People must travel. Imagine that you hold a government job in which you are responsible for making regulations that will protect your country while still allowing reasonable movement of goods and people. Describe the system you would set up to accomplish this.

2. There is a saying "The rich get richer and the poor get poorer." In other words, if you already have money it's easy for you to make more money. However, if you don't have much money, you don't have very many opportunities to change your situation. Poor people don't have access to the tools that might make them rich. Do you think this saying is true? Explain your answer by showing how certain factors (economic, personal, social, etc.) make this statement true or false.

Chapter 3 **Equivalence, Similarity**

This vocabulary may be useful when:
You want to describe kinds of sameness, but you want to go beyond basic terms such as *like, same,* and *similar.*

Key Vocabulary

Group 1	Group 2	Group 3	Group 4	Group 5
equality	parallel	alike	just as	counterpart
parity	echo	identical	likewise	clone
		equivalent		image

✴ Exploring the Vocabulary

Group 1. Nouns for "similar status or position"

equality

Form	Common Related Forms
Noun (uncountable)	*equal* (adjective) *equal* (noun, countable) *equalize* (verb, transitive/intransitive) *equally* (adverb)

In Context 1

The report shows that women still have not achieved equality in the <u>workplace</u>.

In Other Words

The report shows that women still have not come up to the same positions as men in the places where they work.

In Context 2

Because the north has most of the important <u>natural resources</u> there can never be economic equality among the nation's regions.

In Other Words

Because most of the valuable natural things (such as coal or oil or wood) are in the northern part of the nation, the other regions will never be as rich or important as the north.

USAGE CLUES:

- Works well in describing conditions
- Some structures that follow *equality*
    - *of* + a characteristic
    - *in* + a field or an area (see In Context 1)
    - *among* + a group (see In Context 2)
    - *between* + noun phrase(s) naming the two equal things
- Is commonly the object of verbs like *achieve, gain, win, earn, enjoy*
- Is often preceded by an adjective indicating "what kind" (see In Context 2)

parity

Form	Common Related Forms
Noun (uncountable)	None (see also *disparity,* chap. 4)

In Context 1

By <u>adding</u> three fighter squadrons <u>to</u> its air force, the country <u>achieved</u> military parity with its neighbors.

In Other Words

By getting three more groups of fighter airplanes, the country became approximately as strong as other countries near it.

In Context 2

For a while, the Euro slipped below parity with the dollar.

In Other Words

For some time, the value of the Euro was lower than the value of the dollar.

USAGE CLUES:

- Often followed by *with.* The noun phrase after *with* might be the name of something that is considered standard (see In Context 2).
- Has a formal/technical tone. Less widely used than *equality.*
- Commonly used in describing force or strength
- Is often the object of the following verbs: *gain, enjoy*
- Can be preceded by an adjective describing "what kind" (see In Context 1)

 To Help You Remember:

Think of *compare. Parity* implies being equal to a standard. It is related to a term from the game of golf, *par.* This is the "normal" number of strokes—a standard.

Group 2. Verbs meaning "be similar in some ways but under different conditions"

parallel

Form	Common Related Forms
Verb (transitive)	*parallel* (adjective) *parallel* (noun, countable)

In Context 1

Japan's economic downturn in the 1990s paralleled that of the U.S. in the 1980s.

In Other Words

The slowing down of Japan's economy in the 1990s was similar in many ways to what happened in the U.S. during the 1980s.

In Context 2

Dr. Lewis's research at Stanford paralleled Dr. Wu's at the University of Iowa, though neither knew of the other's work.

In Other Words

The research Dr. Lewis did at Stanford was very much like what Dr. Wu was doing at Iowa, but the two did not know about each other's studies.

USAGE CLUES:

- Especially useful for things that occur during some definable period of time (often a long one): events, processes, stories, expressions
- If one thing parallels another, they can happen at different times (see In Context 1) or in different places (see In Context 2).
- The noun form is often followed by *between* (e.g., "parallels between Dr. Lewis's work and Dr. Wu's").
- The adjective form is usually followed by *to* (e.g., "Dr. Lewis's work was parallel to Dr. Wu's").

 To Help You Remember:

The base meaning is "to run beside one another in the same direction without ever meeting." The easiest example is of parallel lines (which travel together but don't cross each other).

parallel lines

Parallel lines

echo

Form	Common Related Forms
Verb (transitive)	*echo* (noun, countable)

In Context 1

America's current "war on drugs" echoes the <u>Prohibition</u> Era of the 1920s.

In Context 2

Tyler's technique of <u>understated</u> surprise echoes the work of Ford Maddox Ford.

In Other Words

America's efforts now to get rid of drugs are similar to the situation in the 1920s, when alcoholic drinks were illegal in the U.S.

In Other Words

The way she surprises readers in a simple, quiet way reminds us of how Ford Maddox Ford wrote.

USAGE CLUES:

- The base meaning refers to the way a sound bounces back after a short time. If you shout in a large, open room with hard walls, your shout will echo— bounce off the walls and come back to you.
- The metaphor is quite strong, so some readers might consider *echo* unsuitable in very technical/formal writing.
- The subject event or situation is always something that happened later than the object event or situation.
- Carries a sense of "reminding one of"
- Works well in contexts of history, literature, art, political science, etc.
- The noun form is usually followed by an *of* phrase (e.g., "There are echoes of Prohibition in the war on drugs").

Consolidation Exercises: Groups 1 and 2

3.1. Collocations. Fill each blank with a word or phrase that goes well with the key term. Several answers are possible in items 4 and 5. *Hint:* Look at the Usage Clues and consider some of the additional vocabulary introduced in this section.

1. The Civil Rights Act of 1964 was intended to give minority groups equality

   _____ whites in all public

   affairs.

2. It would take the U.S. decades to achieve parity _____

   _____ Japan in the production of flat-screen displays.

3. Equality _____ teachers and

   students is impossible. The two are, by definition, unequal.

4. America's huge rise in home prices parallels _____

   _____ .

5. Popular music today echoes _____

   _____ .

3.2. Rephrasing. Using *equality, parity, parallel,* or *echo,* rephrase each of the
      following passages (write it in other words). You may change the form of
      the item you use to fit the grammar of what you write. Change the words
      of the original passage as much as necessary but don't change the meaning.

   1. It would cost hundreds of thousands of dollars to bring our laboratory up to the
      standard of laboratories at other universities.

   2. The Puritans left England for Holland after they realized that their status would
      always be lower than that of other groups within the Church of England.

   3. There are great similarities between the religious art of western South America
      and that of some Pacific Islands.

   4. Some parts of the president's speech last night were similar to statements made
      by John F. Kennedy in 1962.

   5. The process of smithing metal is similar to the process of blowing glass in that
      both involve heating a substance until it can be shaped.

3.3. Meanings and Connections. Next to each description, write the key term that
      best matches it (*equality, parity, parallel,* or *echo*).

   _____ 1. related to lines that go in the same direction but never meet

   _____ 2. related to sounds that bounce back

   _____ 3. related to a standard in the game of golf

Group 3. Adjectives meaning "exactly or almost exactly the same"

alike

Form	Common Related Forms
Adjective	*like* (adjective, attributive) *like* (preposition) *alike* (adverb)

In Context 1

The American robin and the European robin may look alike in their coloring, but they are not the same species of bird.

In Other Words

The two kinds of birds have similar patterns of color, but they are two different kinds of birds.

In Context 2

The new rules will create problems for students and faculty alike.

In Other Words

The new rules will cause problems for both students and teachers.

USAGE CLUES:

- Occurs in two main patterns
  - compound subject + intensive verb (*be, look, seem,* etc.) + *alike* (see In Context 1)
  - pair of noun phrases + *alike* (see In Context 2)
- Often followed by an explanation of how the two things are alike (see In Context 1). This explanation usually starts with *in, because,* or *because of.*
- Notice that *alike* cannot come before the noun(s) it modifies.

identical

Form	Common Related Forms
Adjective	*identity* (noun; uncountable when it means "condition of being the same"; countable when it means "something's/someone's basic nature")

In Context 1

Two clones of the same organism are genetically identical but may look different because of <u>environmental</u> influences.

In Other Words

Two organisms grown artificially from the cells of another will be exactly the same in their genes, but they can look different because they've been influenced by different things in their surroundings.

In Context 2

Singapore's copyright-protection laws are <u>virtually</u> identical to Britain's.

In Other Words

The laws protecting ownership of printed or broadcast ideas in Singapore are almost exactly the same as Britain's.

USAGE CLUES:

- Emphasizes exact similarity—at least in one aspect (see In Context 2)
- Often followed by *to* and the name of one of the similar things
- Can be followed by an *in* phrase that says how (or how much) they are the same
- Sometimes preceded by an adverb that tells how they are similar (see In Context 1)
- Other common adverbs are *virtually, almost, practically*—indicating that the similarity is not exact but any differences are very small and meaningless (see In Context 2)

As They Say

Six of one, half dozen of the other.

No matter which choice you make the result will be the same.

A dozen = 12, so a "half dozen" = 6.

For example:

A: Would it be better to stay at the Wilton Hotel or the Crescent?
B: Six of one, half dozen of the other.

Speaker B is saying that it doesn't matter which hotel they stay at, because the experience will be very much the same at either place.

equivalent

Form	Common Related Forms
Adjective	*equivalence* (noun meaning "the quality or condition of being equal," usually uncountable) *equivalent* (noun meaning "something that is equal to another," usually countable)

In Context 1

To be <u>admitted</u> to this school you need a score of 220 on a test called the MLLE or an equivalent score on various other tests.

In Context 2

A British A-level qualification is roughly equivalent to an American high school diploma.

In Other Words

To become a student at this school you need an MLLE score of 220 or some other test score that indicates the same level of ability.

In Other Words

Someone completing an A level in Britain has done work similar to that done by someone who completes high school in the U.S.

USAGE CLUES:

- Implies "not exactly the same but having the same value or same purpose"
- Often followed by a *to* phrase to name one of the similar items (see In Context 2)
- Works well in describing positions, values, amounts, scores, or achievements
- The noun form *equivalent* is often followed by an *of* phrase (e.g., "An A-level qualification is the equivalent of a high school diploma").

Group 4. Adverbs indicating similarity

just as

Form	Common Related Forms
Subordinator (introducing an adverbial clause)	None

In Context 1

Just as a dog obeys its master, a wolf <u>defers to</u> the <u>leader of the pack</u>.

In Context 2

<u>Glaciers</u> may look <u>stationary</u> but they <u>flow</u>, just as rivers do.

In Other Words

The way a wolf follows the instructions of its group leader is similar to the way a dog obeys the human who cares for it.

In Other Words

Even though glaciers (large, thick sheets of ice on top of land) look like they aren't moving, they move downhill in the same way rivers do.

USAGE CLUES:

- Always comes at the beginning of an adverbial clause (see In Context 1 and 2). Therefore, the clause it introduces cannot be the only one in the sentence.
- *BE CAREFUL:* DO NOT follow this with a simple noun phrase. For example, *"just as wolves, dogs need to belong to a group" is wrong. Fix it by adding a verb (e.g., "just as wolves do . . .") or changing *just as* to *like* (e.g., "like wolves, dogs . . .").
- *BE CAREFUL: Just as* also has a different meaning related to time: "at exactly the same time."

likewise

Form	Common Related Forms
Adverbial	None

In Context 1

Push factors such as war or <u>famine</u> are notorious for causing great population shifts. Likewise, pull factors such as economic opportunity can lead to <u>large-scale</u> immigration.

In Context 2

A stalk of grass, of course, remains non-woody and <u>withers</u> after producing seed. The banana does likewise, and this makes it technically an <u>herb</u>.

In Other Words

War or widespread hunger can cause lots of people to move to other places. So can "pull factors" like the chance to make money in other places.

In Other Words

The upright part of a grass plant does not become like wood, and it dries up and dies after the plant produces seed. The banana plant does the same thing, so the banana is technically an herb.

---

*An asterisk indicates incorrect usage.

USAGE CLUES:

- Can be a sentence modifier, in two main positions
    - at the beginning of a sentence (see In Context 1)
    - after the subject
- As the modifier of a verb
- If the verb is an operator or a pro-verb (*do, have, be*), *likewise* comes after it, not before it.
- *Do/did likewise* is very common (see In Context 2).
- Often positioned between
    - *be* and a participle or simple adjective (e.g., "These birds are likewise interesting"; "Our department is likewise eager to . . ."). This sounds somewhat old-fashioned or formal.
    - *have* and a participle ("They have likewise insisted . . .")

 To Help You Remember:

Is a short form of an older English phrase *in like wise*, meaning "in a similar way"

⬚ Consolidation Exercises: Groups 3 and 4

3.4. Collocations. Fill each blank with a word or phrase that goes well with the key vocabulary item. There are several possible answers for items 2, 4, and 5.
Hint: Look at the Usage Clues and consider some of the additional vocabulary introduced in this section.

1. It's the kind of movie that appeals to young and _____

    _____ alike.

2. Just as _____, men often find

    themselves unwanted for certain jobs just because they're men.

3. A temperature of –40°C is equivalent _____

    _____ a temperature of –40°F.

4. Although they have different names, the FTE test and the MLLE test are

    _____ identical.

5. The FTE asks test takers to _____

    _____. The MLLE likewise requires some essay writing.

3.5. Rephrasing. Using *alike, identical, equivalent, just as,* or *likewise,* rephrase each of the following passages (write it in other words). You may change the form of the item you use to fit the grammar of what you write. Change the words of the original passage as much as necessary but don't change the meaning.

1. Flat-screen displays make laptop computers possible. They also make it possible to install an individual television monitor at each seat of an airplane.

2. Mohandas Gandhi urged nonviolent resistance to injustice. So did Martin Luther King, Jr.

3. The Great Plains of North America and the steppes of Asia are both temperate-zone grasslands.

4. Even though some U.S "silver dollars" are not actually made of silver, they have the same face value as those that are pure silver.

5. Even though English and Hindi are very different, they come from the same ancient tongue, Proto-Indo-European.

Group 5. Nouns for "things that are similar in some way"

counterpart

Form	Common Related Forms
Noun (countable)	None

In Context 1

Minnesota's Jesperson was in daily contact with her counterpart at Iowa State.

In Context 2

There's no counterpart to the U.S. Senate in the Malindian parliament.

In Other Words

Jesperson, who worked for the University of Minnesota, spoke every day with the person at Iowa State who had a job similar to hers.

In Other Words

In the Malindian parliament, there's no group similar to the U.S. Senate.

USAGE CLUES:

- Usually refers to people, groups, or institutions
- Useful in discussing jobs or positions in different organizations or systems
- To name one of the similar items, you can use an *of* phrase or a *to* phrase (see In Context 2).

 To Help You Remember:

The word part *counter* often means "against." A counterpart is a "part" (or party) that would stand next to (against) some other. Think of matching things from different columns, where an item in one column has a counterpart (something to "stand against" it) in the other column.

Greek	Roman
K	K
Λ	L
M	M
N	N

The Roman character L is the counterpart of the Greek character Λ.

clone

Form	Common Related Forms
Noun (countable)	*clone* (verb, transitive) *cloning* (noun, uncountable)

In Context 1

Everyone in the office had short hair and wore dark blue suits, as if they were all clones of their boss.

In Other Words

Everyone in the office had hairstyles and clothes that made them look like exact copies of their boss.

In Context 2

Renton's new <u>novel</u> is just another *Scarlet Letter* clone.

In Other Words

Renton's new book is not very original. It is very much like *The Scarlet Letter* (a novel by Nathaniel Hawthorne).

USAGE CLUES:

- The basic meaning is "an organism made by artificially copying the genetic material of an original."
- Informal tone. Often indicates a bad opinion of the thing called "a clone," because a clone is not original and originality is considered good (see In Context 1).
- Often followed by an *of* phrase to name the original from which others are copied (see In Context 1)
- Often, a noun phrase naming the original comes before *clone* (see In Context 2).
- The object of the verb *clone* is usually the original (e.g., "They cloned the program" means "They made a copy of the program"). If the object noun is followed by a *from* phrase, the direct object is the copy, and the object of *from* is the original (e.g., "They cloned a new program from Basecorp's best-selling Powerdata software").

 To Help You Remember:

Comes from a Greek root meaning "to cut." Cloning originally referred to growing a new plant from a piece that had been cut from an existing plant.

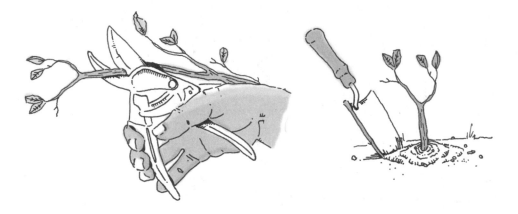

image

Form	Common Related Forms
Noun (countable but usually singular)	None in this meaning

In Context 1

The team's research <u>design</u> was the image of an earlier project at Stanford.

In Context 2

The Pandas are a roots-<u>reggae</u> band in Marley's image.

In Other Words

The plan for the structure of the team's research was exactly like one used in an earlier project at Stanford.

In Other Words

The Pandas play traditional reggae music (a style associated with the island of Jamaica). Their performance style reminds people of Marley's.

USAGE CLUES:

- More neutral than *clone*
- Appears in two main patterns, each of which is a definite noun phrase
    the image of (see In Context 1)
    possessive + *image* (see In Context 2), often preceded by *in*
- Often occurs in an informal phrase "the spitting image" meaning "something so much like the original that it's hard to see any difference between the two"

Consolidation Exercises: Group 5

3.6. Collocations. Fill each blank with a word or phrase that goes well with the key vocabulary item. There are several possible answers for item 1. *Hint:* Look at the Usage Clues and consider some of the additional vocabulary introduced in this section.

1. Some people have said that the new president is just a(n) _____

    _____ clone.

2. The Topscreen TV was so popular that dozens of companies rushed to create

    products _____ its image.

3. Even though both receive some public money, PBS is not really the American counterpart _____ Britain's BBC.

4. To some degree the Mounties are the FBI's counterpart _____

_____ Canadian law enforcement.

3.7. Rephrasing. Use *counterpart, clone,* or *image* to rephrase each of the following passages (to write it in other words). You may change the form of the item to fit the grammar of what you write. Change the words of the original passage as much as necessary but don't change the meaning.

1. Robertson is not a very original leader. Almost all of her policies and actions are like Mayor LaGuardia's.

2. The Inland Revenue Authority of Singapore performs the same functions there that the Internal Revenue Service performs in the U.S.

3. The original plans for the town of New Hartford were that its street layout should be exactly like the layout in Hartford, Connecticut.

4. The new X-IS computer is an exact copy of the Portway 2100 system.

5. Todd Wilson is in charge of quality control at Dobson Hydraulics. Marla Spreese does that job at MNO Hydraulics.

👁 Comprehensive Review Exercises

3.8. Matching. Next to each item in the left column, write the letter of the best definition/description from the right column. Do not use any letter more than once.

____ 1. equality
____ 2. parallel
____ 3. parity
____ 4. echo
____ 5. alike
____ 6. identical
____ 7. equivalent
____ 8. just as
____ 9. likewise
____ 10. counterpart
____ 11. clone
____ 12. image

a. means "not the same but having the same value"
b. something not very original because it's just a copy of something else
c. is similar to something that came earlier
d. "in the same way"; can join two clauses within a sentence
e. "in the same way"; cannot join two clauses within a sentence
f. someone/something with the same job as someone else in a different organization
g. be very much the same as another process or situation in a different time or place
h. something with the same "appearance"
i. adjective meaning "the same"; cannot come before the noun it modifies
j. condition of being the same as some standard or level
k. "exactly the same" but often preceded by adverbs (*virtually, practically*) that mean "almost"
l. the condition of having the same status; works well in contexts about society

3.9. Fitting In. Choose the best word or phrase to complete each sentence. Write it in the blank.

> *Example:* Because of the heavy rain, we had to <u>alter</u> our plans. (mutate, transform, alter)

1. For years Reshko Platters has lagged behind the industry's production average, but analysts predict it will soon achieve _____

   with its competitors. (parity, identity, equality)

2. High oil prices threaten the economy. Labor shortages, _____

   _____, could end the economic boom. (just as, likewise, alike)

3. The people known as the "Tinkers" are the Irish _____

   _____ of America's Rom. (parallel, clone, counterpart)

4. Senator Keel's racist remarks _____ certain pro-

nouncements by Adolf Hitler. (are alike, echo, are images of)

5. Student demonstrations in Paris in 1968 _____

campus unrest at the same time in the U.S. (echoed, paralleled, were identical)

6. In most societies that don't use money, people barter—exchange goods and

services that are roughly _____ in value. (alike,

equivalent, identical)

3.10. Combinations and Collocations. Fill in each blank with a word or phrase that
fits well with the key vocabulary item. Many answers are possible for most
items.

1. Despite decades of effort, women have still not _____

_____ equality with men in a lot of fields.

2. The Williams and Frey research designs are alike _____

_____ each requires two interviewers per subject.

3. The human body carries electrical current just as copper wire _____

_____ .

4. Hillcomp's personal organizer is a clone _____

the Organix palmtop.

5. A normal water molecule and a deuterium (or "heavy water") molecule are

_____ identical, differing in only one atom.

6. The Sudanese famine of 1997 echoed _____ a

decade earlier.

7. During the so-called cold war there was rough parity _____

_____ the U.S. and the Soviet Union.

Additional Vocabulary for Chapter 3

The additional words and phrases that have come up in the In Context examples in chapter 3 can be found in Appendix 1. (They are underlined when they occur in the In Context sections.) These terms are not fully explained, but you should be able to understand them from the contexts and brief explanations that are given. Do the exercises below to help solidify your understanding of these words and phrases.

3.11.   Additional Vocabulary 1: Meanings. In each blank, write the letter of the meaning from column B that goes best with each vocabulary item in Column A.

Column A
_____ 1. defer to
_____ 2. wither
_____ 3. flow
_____ 4. create
_____ 5. Prohibition
_____ 6. design
_____ 7. robin
_____ 8. natural resources
_____ 9. environmental
_____ 10. famine
_____ 11. virtually
_____ 12. novel

Column B
a. trees, metals, water, and other useful things found in nature
b. become weaker, drier, and smaller, like a plant that might die
c. a situation in which large numbers of people don't have enough to eat
d. to move, like water going downhill
e. a kind of book
f. a species of bird
g. a system under which it was illegal to drink alcohol in the U.S.
h. follow the instructions of
i. related to the conditions or things around you
j. make
k. almost; for all practical purposes
l. a plan for the structure of something

3.12.   Additional Vocabulary 2: Fitting into Sentences. Fill in each blank on page 64 with one of the additional vocabulary items from the list below. Do not use any item more than once. Some items will not be used at all.

achieve	glacier	species
add to	herb	stationary
admit	large-scale	understated
create	natural resources	workplace
defer to	Prohibition	
faculty	reggae	

1. Japan's shockingly bright pink-and-neon pachinko parlors contrast with the
   _____ colors of other buildings nearby.

2. For most of human history, people believed that the Earth was
   _____ and that the sun moved around it.

3. Excessive noise in the _____ can be a major
   problem for factory workers.

4. The genus *Escherichia* includes several _____
   of bacteria, the best known being *E. coli.*

5. Wilson has had a hard time at work, and his troubles at home _____
   _____ an already tough situation.

6. Some people _____ success through hard work,
   but others get it through pure good luck.

7. A(n) _____ prevention program, in which
   doctors vaccinated at least 120,000 people, kept the virus from spreading.

8. The University of Western Superior won't _____
   _____ any applicant with an entry test score below 850.

9. When a(n) _____ reaches the sea, large chunks
   of ice break off it and fall into the water.

10. Mr. Greenboro joined the school's _____ in
    1974 and has taught history and math since then.

11. You're the expert, so the rest of us will _____
    you. Tell us what to do, and we'll do it.

12. The storm _____ enormous waves that
    destroyed several seaside towns.

▌▌ Writing Projects

3.13. Writing Projects. The following are some suggestions for writing projects that will allow you to use the key vocabulary and some of the additional vocabulary. Each of the topics could be lightly covered in an essay of 500–600 words or more thoroughly in a paper of 1,500–2,000 words. To write information-packed longer papers you should do some research in the library and/or on the Internet. *Note:* It may feel more natural in your essay for you to discuss differences as well as similarities. Please feel free to do so. (For help with vocabulary about differences see chap. 4.)

1. In the United States and many other countries, teachers do not earn as much money as other people with similar levels of education. Also, teachers do not enjoy a very high social position. Answer one of the following questions related to this situation.
   (a) Why in your opinion, do societies not value teachers as highly as other people with similar levels of education? (Choose this one ONLY if you agree that this is true.)
   (b) What could be done to help improve teachers' salaries and social position?
2. Artificial materials are widely used in place of natural materials. Plastics and other factory-produced materials may look like (and be used in place of) more natural materials such as glass, leather, stone, wood, metal, and many others. Consider some large, complex machine or object—a car, a building, etc.— and write about the artificial materials used in its construction. You might want to consider such issues as these: Why are artificial materials used instead of natural ones? How would the machine or object be better or worse if only natural materials had been used?
3. The most common situation for writing about similarities is when those similarities are surprising or unexpected. Choose two places or situations you know very well—two that most people might expect to be very different—and discuss some interesting or unexpected similarities between them.

Chapter 4   Difference, Inequality

This vocabulary may be useful when:
You want to describe the ways in which things are NOT the same, but you want to go beyond using *different, difference,* or comparative adjective phrases with *less* or *not as.*

Key Vocabulary

Group 1	Group 2	Group 3
disparity	differ	differentiate
inequality	diverge	distinguish

Group 4	Group 5	Group 6
discrete	heterogeneous	contrast
disparate	diverse	discrepancy
		gap

✴ Exploring the Vocabulary

Group 1. Nouns meaning "difference in amount or position"

disparity

Form	Common Related Forms
Noun (countable)	None

In Context 1

The disparity between a teacher's pay and that of other certified professionals is huge.

In Context 2

Amanda Huggins dedicated her <u>career</u> to correcting the disparities in service among the agency's clients—disparities usually based on race.

In Other Words

There is a very large difference between the amount of money a teacher earns and the amount that any other professional whose work requires a license would earn.

In Other Words

Amanda Huggins spent most of her working life correcting situations in which the agency gave people of some races much worse service than it gave people of other races.

USAGE CLUES:

- Often followed by a *between* or *among* phrase to name the things that are different (see In Context 1 and 2)
- An *in* phrase describing the area of difference may follow it (see In Context 2).
- Often used to discuss social or economic conditions
- If you eliminate unequal conditions you *correct* a disparity.
- An adjective of size or degree—*huge, enormous, great, significant*—often appears with *disparity* (see In Context 1).
- Unlike *inequality,* is not usually preceded by an adjective naming the kind of disparity (e.g., ??"social disparity"?? is less likely than "social inequality")

 To Help You Remember:

Is the negative form of the noun *parity* (see chap. 3), which comes from a Latin root meaning "equality; being level or even with." *Dis-* means "not," so disparity is "NOT being on the same level." The Latin root is also the root of the golf term *par,* which means "a normal or average score."

inequality

Form	Common Related Forms
Noun (usually uncountable)	*unequal* (adjective) *Note:* There is no such word as *inequal.*

In Context 1

There is a <u>disturbing</u> inequality in the way the police <u>respond</u> to calls from people of different races.

In Context 2

The inequality among test scores of <u>otherwise</u> similar students is <u>puzzling</u>.

In Other Words

The police answer a call from a person of one race very differently from the way they respond to a call from a person of another race. This difference is something we should worry about.

In Other Words

It's very hard to understand why students who are similar in most ways had such different test scores.

USAGE CLUES:

- Can be followed by a *between* or *among* phrase to name the things that are different (see In Context 2)
- An *in* phrase often states the area of difference (see In Context 1).
- Works well in contexts about society and employment and in other contexts about human relations
- Usually uncountable (meaning "condition" or "state") but sometimes countable (when it means "a kind of dissimilarity between two amounts or positions" or "an occasion when there is dissimilarity between two amounts or positions")
- There is also a technical meaning in mathematics: "a mathematical expression showing that two quantities are not equal" (e.g., "$a < b$").

Group 2. Intransitive verbs meaning "be different"

differ

Form	Common Related Forms
Verb (intransitive)	*difference* (noun, countable) *different* (adjective) *differently* (adverb) See also entry for *differentiate* (below).

In Context 1

The DNA sequence of chimpanzees and that of humans differ by only a few nucleic acid pairs.

In Context 2

European socialists differed from their African counterparts in their <u>distaste</u> for true <u>revolution</u>.

In Other Words

A few pairs of nucleic acids are not the same in a chimpanzee as they are in a human, but in other ways the DNA patterns of the two are the same.

In Other Words

Unlike African socialists, European socialists did not really want to get rid of their current governments.

USAGE CLUES:

- The most important word to learn in this meaning area. If you can use this correctly, you can write about almost any kind of situation in which things are not the same.
- Some common structures to follow *differ*
  - *in* to name area of difference (see In Context 2)
  - *from* to name one of the different things (see In Context 2)
  - *by* to describe the extent of the difference (see In Context 1)
- Often has a compound subject (see In Context 1)
- Can usually be replaced by "be different." Doing so makes the passage sound a bit less formal.
- *BE CAREFUL: Differ* also has another meaning, "disagree with an opinion."

diverge

Form	Common Related Forms
Verb (intransitive)	*divergence* (noun, uncountable) *divergent* (adjective)

In Context 1

From the graph, you can see that tax revenue and infrastructure spending diverge after 1994.

In Other Words

The graph has a line showing how much money the government took in from taxes and another line showing how much the government spent on basic services like roads and water supply. The two lines run near each other for a while but then start separating at the point on the graph that shows 1994.

In Context 2

I agree that guns should be controlled, but I'm afraid my views diverge from yours when it comes to confiscating guns from innocent citizens.

In Other Words

We both agree that guns should be controlled, but I don't think (as you do) that the government should take guns away from people who have never committed a crime.

USAGE CLUES:

- Creates an image of motion, of going separate ways, so it works best with things that can be thought of as "moving in some direction," such as lines (or what lines represent), trends, opinions, or processes
- Appropriate only when things were once similar but the similarity began weakening.
- The subject is often a plural noun (see In Context 2) or a compound of two or more noun phrases (see In Context 1).
- If the subject is *not* compound, *diverge* could be followed by a *from* phrase that names one of the "different" things.

 To Help You Remember:

Comes from a Latin root meaning "bend away (from each other)." Things that diverge bend away and move along different paths.

Group 3. Verbs that can mean "create a difference or notice a difference"

differentiate

Form	Common Related Forms
Verb (transitive/intransitive)	*differentiation* (noun, usually uncountable) *differentiated* (verbal adjective)

In Context 1: "create a difference"

(a) Color differentiates the two types of mushroom.
(b) Color differentiates one mushroom from the other.

In Other Words

The two kinds of mushroom are similar in many ways, but you can tell them apart by their color.

In Context 2: "notice or perceive a difference"

(a) It's hard for me to differentiate between Bach's style and Telemann's.
(b) It's hard for me to differentiate Bach's style from Telemann's.

In Other Words

I have a hard time hearing differences between the musical style of Johann Sebastian Bach and that of Georg Philipp Telemann.

USAGE CLUES:

- Works best when things are similar in many ways but different in a few important ways

In Context 1 ("create a difference")

- Is always transitive
- The subject is a characteristic or an attribute that makes the difference.
- Possible object patterns
     a plural noun phrase (see item (a))
     a noun phrase naming an unusual thing + *from* + another noun phrase naming the things it's different from

In Context 2 ("notice or perceive a difference")

- The subject is a person or group of people.
- Can be transitive (see item (b)). In these cases, the object pattern is as follows: noun phrase naming one thing + *from* + another noun phrase naming the thing it's different from.
- Can also be intransitive (see item (a)). In these cases, the verb is followed by a *between* or *among* phrase.

As They Say

   apples and oranges

Things so basically different that it doesn't make sense to compare them

For example:

A: Widaya sings a lot better than DeKorne.

B: But that's apples and oranges. DeKorne's an actor, not a singer.

Speaker B is saying it's not fair to compare Widaya's singing with DeKorne's because DeKorne can't be expected to sing well.

distinguish

Form	Common Related Forms
Verb (usually transitive/ sometimes intransitive)	*distinct* (adjective meaning "easily seen because it stands out from the group") *distinctive* (adjective meaning "easily recognized and usually better than average") *distinction* (noun; usually uncountable, meaning either "the process of making something stand out" or "the condition in which something stands out from the crowd"; can also be countable, meaning "characteristics that make something different from others of its kind")

In Context 1: "make something different"

(a) Financial <u>savvy</u> distinguished Barnard from earlier governors.
(b) Light weight and low radiation distinguish the Apex 4000 cellular phone.

In Other Words

(a) Barnard was different from earlier governors in that she knew a lot about managing money.
(b) The Apex 4000 is different (from other cellular phones) because it weighs less and emits less radiation.

In Context 2: "see or perceive a difference"

(a) Fog and darkness made it hard for us to distinguish humans from trees.
(b) With enough training, you can learn to distinguish among the many varieties of maple tree.

In Other Words

(a) Because of the fog and darkness, it was hard for us to see clearly enough to know which objects were trees and which were people.
(b) If you study enough about maple trees, you can learn to tell the differences among various kinds.

USAGE CLUES:

In Context 1 ("make something different")

- The subject is always a characteristic that makes the object different. This is very often a *good* characteristic.
- A common object pattern: direct object + *from* + another noun phrase (see item (a))

- If there is only a direct object (with no *from* phrase), it implies "from all others of its type" (item (b)).
- Often in the passive (e.g., "Barnard was distinguished from earlier governors by her financial savvy")

In Context 2 ("see or perceive a difference")

- The subject is a human, a group of humans, or some other entity capable of sensing (e.g., a camera, microphone, etc.).
- For the transitive form, here are some common object patterns:
  a direct object followed by a *from* phrase (see item (a)).
  a direct object that is a compound noun phrase (with *and*)
- The intransitive form is almost always followed by a *between* or *among* phrase (see item (b)).
- *Note:* Before a noun, the verbal adjective *distinguished*—as in *a distinguished leader*—has a different meaning, "famous and dignified."

Consolidation Exercises: Groups 1, 2, and 3

4.1. Collocations. Fill each blank with a word or phrase that goes well with the key vocabulary item. For item 2, there are several possible answers. *Hint:* Look at the Usage Clues and consider some of the additional vocabulary introduced in this section.

1. I'm afraid that the interests of our accounting department sometimes diverge

   _____ the larger goals of the company.

2. We have to try to _____ the disparity between the

   educational standards in our city schools and those in the suburbs.

3. There's a huge disparity _____ rainfall amounts in

   North Dakota _____ in Minnesota.

4. The radioactive isotope of the element differs _____

   _____ the base form _____ only two neutrons.

5. A certain self-assurance distinguishes Hillaire _____

   _____ the other candidates.

6. The best ways to differentiate _____ the many

    species of lemur are by the fur coloring and by the shape of the paw.

4.2. Rephrasing. Using *disparity, inequality, differ, diverge, differentiate,* or
     distinguish, rephrase each of the following passages (write it in other words).
     You may change the form of the item you use to fit the grammar of what you
     write. Change the words of the original passage as much as necessary but
     don't change the meaning.

    1. The planets known as gas giants are not the same as the other planets because
       they don't have actual surfaces.

    2. After the company was split up, the various divisions pursued different
       marketing plans.

    3. Management promised a lot more to the workers than was ever actually
       delivered.

    4. Members of the Govanese minority don't have as much access to government
       services as other citizens have.

    5. You can't expect customers in Africa, where incomes are relatively low, to pay
       the same for a CD as customers in North America do.

    6. Traditionally, the most important difference between Cajun music and zydeco
       was whether the performers were of European or African ancestry.

    7. We need judges who can tell the difference between truly dangerous criminals
       and basically good people who have simply made a mistake.

Group 4. Adjectives meaning "separate; standing apart"

discrete

Form	Common Related Forms
Adjective	*discretely* (adverb) *discreteness* (noun, uncountable) is possible.

In Context 1

Phonetics students must learn to break a stream of speech down into discrete sounds.

In Context 2

The two companies were discrete from one another, despite having a common <u>parent</u> <u>company</u>.

In Other Words

Students learning about the sounds of language have to know how to separate a long piece of connected speech into separate, individual sounds.

In Other Words

The two companies were totally separate from each other even though they were both owned by the same larger company.

USAGE CLUES:

- Often used to describe units, parts, or pieces
- Often occurs in the context of "breaking" or "dividing" (see In Context 1)
- Not appropriate to describe a living thing as a whole but can refer to parts of living things (*discrete cells, discrete branches*)
- Most commonly comes before the noun it modifies
- When *discrete* comes *after* the noun it modifies, it is very often followed by a *from* phrase (see In Context 2).
- *BE CAREFUL:* Do not confuse with *discreet* ("tactful"), which sounds the same but is spelled differently. Also, do not associate it with *discreet*'s other forms (*discretion, discreetly*).

disparate

Form	Common Related Forms
Adjective	*disparately* (adverb) *Note: disparity* is NOT a form of *disparate*. See comments on *disparity* earlier in this section.

In Context 1

<u>Attending to</u> the disparate needs of the community after the <u>tornado</u> was a <u>massive</u> undertaking.

In Context 2

Because disparate broadcast formats are used worldwide, a TV from one country will not necessarily work in another.

In Other Words

Taking care of the many different things the community needed after the tornado (a violent windstorm) struck was a huge job.

In Other Words

Because the countries of the world broadcast their television programs in many different formats, a TV made in one country might not work in another country.

USAGE CLUES:

- The base meaning is "numerous and very different."
- Can imply "hard to bring together"
- Often used to describe groups, systems, organizations, parts or members of a group, requirements or demands
- Almost always comes before the noun it modifies

 To Help You Remember:

Comes from Latin roots meaning "prepared differently." (Notice that the word part *-parate* is familiar from *separate*.) Disparate things come from different sources or backgrounds, reflecting "different preparations."

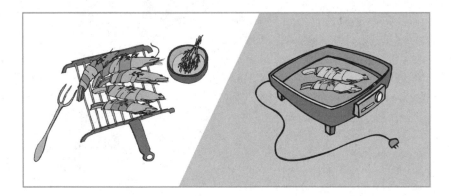

Group 5. Adjectives meaning "different in origin or kind"

heterogeneous

Form	Common Related Forms
Adjective	*heterogeneity* (noun, uncountable)

In Context 1

India is linguistically heterogeneous, being home to tongues from several distinct families.

In Context 2

Labor organizers found the heterogeneous construction workers very difficult to unionize.

In Other Words

In India there are many different kinds of languages, from many different basic groups of languages.

In Other Words

People who try to create organizations of workers had a hard time getting the construction workers to form a group, because there were too many differences among the workers.

USAGE CLUES:

- Works especially well when you want to emphasize that differences within a group are very basic, not just related to surface characteristics
- Often comes before nouns for groups of things or people (e.g., *collection, group, society*)
- Especially common in discussing groups of living things and their members
- Can come either before the noun it modifies (see In Context 2) or after a linking verb (see In Context 1)
- Has a commonly used opposite, *homogeneous,* meaning "all of the same type"

diverse

Form	Common Related Forms
Adjective	*diversity* (noun, uncountable)
	diversify (verb, transitive/intransitive)
	NOT in this meaning: *diversion*

In Context 1

Government <u>regulations</u> encouraged the university to hire a diverse teaching force.

In Other Words

Rules set by the government led the university to hire teachers of many different races, nationalities, and other characteristics.

In Context

The <u>obstacles</u> to the research were diverse, ranging from <u>lack</u> of funds to complaints that the research was <u>immoral</u>.

In Other Words

Many different things—from not enough money to complaints by people who thought it was wrong to do such research—made the research difficult.

USAGE CLUES:

- Often used to mean "various in a *good* way"—especially for social groups (see In Context 1)
- Commonly used to describe groups of people, parts of a system, settings or locations, statements, reasons, styles, and other things that can represent a wide range
- The verb form *diversify* can mean either "make something represent a wider number of different characteristics" (a transitive meaning) or "become more different" (an intransitive meaning).
- A common use of the transitive form of *diversify* is in describing investments or things you own. To *diversify your* <u>portfolio</u> is to make your group of investments include many different kinds of shares, bonds, etc.
- The noun *diversity* is often followed by an *in* phrase (+ an uncountable or singular mass noun) or *among* phrase (+ a plural countable noun) to name the group that is diverse (e.g., "diversity among its employees").

 To Help You Remember:

Comes from Latin roots meaning "turned in different directions." Imagine a number of lines, each going in a slightly different direction. The lines make up a diverse group.

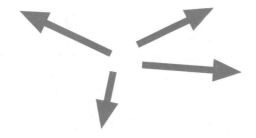

⧉ Consolidation Exercises: Groups 4 and 5

4.3. Collocations. Fill each blank with a word or phrase that goes well with the key vocabulary item (or related form). There is only one correct answer for item 2. There are several possible answers for items 1, 3, 4, and 5. *Hint:* Look at the Usage Clues and consider some of the additional vocabulary introduced in this section.

1. Gavin put together a heterogeneous _____ of timepieces—watches, hourglasses, even water clocks.

2. To create more diversity _____ the student body, the university began offering courses in non-Western literature and in Asian and African music.

3. The two companies, with their disparate _____, had a hard time integrating their operations after the merger.

4. Before you can understand the computer network as a whole, you have to be able to think of it as a collection of discrete _____.

5. The more diverse a(n) _____ is, the better it can survive drought, floods, fire, disease, or infestation by insects.

4.4. Rephrasing. Using *discrete, disparate, heterogeneous,* or *diverse,* rephrase each of the following passages (write it in other words). You may change the form of the item you use to fit the grammar of what you write. Change the words of the original passage as much as necessary but don't change the meaning.

1. When you look at a leaf with your naked eye, you see a smooth, unbroken surface. When you look at it through a microscope, however, you can see lots of small, individual cells.

2. During his first year as governor, Noonan was frustrated by his inability to find common interests among the very different ethnic groups in the state.

3. Because most of the families in the Onawanda School District were of similar backgrounds, the students at the school weren't exposed to different languages, religious beliefs, or cultural practices.

4. On the shelves of Professor Gardenia's office was a mixture of many different objects, representing travels through Europe, Asia, and South America.

5. Many visitors to New Zealand are surprised by the different types of ecosystems on the islands—with semiarid grasslands, coastal plains, and alpine meadows often only a few miles from one another.

Group 6. Nouns meaning "difference in general"

contrast

Form	Common Related Forms
Noun (countable)	*contrast* (verb; intransitive when it means "be different from"; transitive when it means "mention a difference between/among things") *contrasting* (verbal adjective) *contrastive* (adjective)

In Context 1

There was a sharp contrast between life before the oil <u>boom</u> and life afterward.

In Other Words

The way people lived in this area before they began getting a lot of money from oil was greatly different from the way they lived later, and the differences were very clear.

In Context 2

In contrast to its neighbors, Bangsa refused to bring in foreign workers to solve its labor shortage.

In Other Words

Unlike other nearby countries, Bangsa would not import a lot of workers from other countries to make up for a lack of local workers.

USAGE CLUES:

- Implies a difference that is easy to see, hear, etc.
- Some common adjectives that go with *contrast: clear, sharp, great* (see In Context 1)
- Very often followed by a *between . . . and* structure or *among*. These phrases name the items that are different from each other (see In Context 1).
- Often occurs in the phrase *in contrast (to)*—a common discourse marker showing difference (see In Context 2)
- The intransitive verb *contrast* is often followed by *with* (e.g., "Life after the oil boom contrasts sharply with life before") .
- A common way of paraphrasing *contrasts with* is *stands in sharp contrast with/to* (e.g., "Life after the oil boom stands in sharp contrast with life before").

discrepancy

Form	Common Related Forms
Noun (countable)	No related forms are common. There is an adjective *discrepant*, but it's rarely used.

In Context 1

There was a huge discrepancy between his hopes and his abilities.

In Other Words

He hoped to be able to do many more things than he was actually able to do.

In Context 2

The <u>auditors</u> discovered a discrepancy between the company's financial reports and its bank records.

In Other Words

The people who examine accounts discovered a big difference between the amount of money the company claimed to have and the amount it actually had in the bank.

USAGE CLUES:

- The basic meaning is "(undesirable) difference in value or amount."
- Notice that *discrepancy* implies an undesirable situation. Things would be better if the discrepancy did not exist.

- Works well in contexts of statements, claims, promises, accounts
- Often followed by a *between* phrase
- Often preceded by an adjective of size (*huge, vast, large, small, tiny*)

 To Help You Remember:

Comes from a Latin root meaning "make sounds that don't harmonize." If there is a discrepancy, two things fit poorly together, like two musical notes that don't sound good together.

gap

Form	Common Related Forms
Noun (countable)	None

In Context 1

There was a large gap between the government's spending and its <u>income</u>.

In Other Words

The amount of money the government took in was not very close to the amount it spent.

In Context 2

<u>Negotiators</u> worked hard to close the gap between the two sides' positions.

In Other Words

People trying to get the two sides to agree had to work very hard to eliminate the differences between one side's ideas and the ideas of the other side.

USAGE CLUES:

- Because it is metaphorical (it calls up an image of a large hole or an empty space), it has a slightly informal tone. It works well in most academic writing but would not be appropriate in a very formal piece.
- Often followed by a *between* phrase (see In Context 1 and 2)
- Some common expressions in which *gap* is the direct object of a verb: "*create a gap*," "*bridge* the gap," "*close* the gap" (see In Context 2)
- Very useful in discussing different viewpoints, positions, or circumstances—things that could be similar but aren't

 To Help You Remember:

The base meaning is "empty space." This base meaning comes up in a lot of cases, such as "a gap in one's teeth," "a gap between mountains," etc.

Consolidation Exercises: Group 6

4.5. Collocations. Fill each blank with a word or phrase that goes well with the key vocabulary item. There are several possible answers to items 2, 3, and 4. *Hint:* Look at the Usage Clues and consider some of the additional vocabulary introduced in this section.

1. Time-zone differences account for the discrepancy _____

   _____ the date on this form and what she told us.

2. There's a(n) _____ contrast between the flat

   western shore of Lake Michigan and the hilly, dune-studded eastern shore.

3. Giving government-owned land to newly freed slaves did a lot to _____

   _____ the social gap between former slaves and slaveholders.

4. Educational differences have _____ a huge

   economic gap between the residents of Loomis City and those from nearby

   suburbs.

4.6. Rephrasing. Using *contrast, discrepancy,* or *gap,* rephrase each of the following passages (write it in other words). You may change the form of the item you use to fit the grammar of what you write. Change the words of the original passage as much as necessary but don't change the meaning.

1. At Fastridge High School, the athletes get a lot of special attention and enjoy a very different life from that which nonathletes live.

2. The cars in the executive parking area at Fukuichi Systems are very expensive, and it's easy to notice the difference between these and the old, falling-apart cars parked in other areas of the lot.

3. Livia says she got home by about 10:30, but several of her friends claim she was at the nightclub until at least midnight.

4. We expected to begin making a profit after about 18 months, but even after three years we're still posting a loss every quarter.

👁 **Comprehensive Review Exercises**

4.7. Matching. Next to each item in the left column, write the letter of the best meaning/description from the right column. Do not use any letter more than once.

____	1. disparity	a. means "made up of many different kinds"
____	2. discrete	b. in its basic meaning means "empty space"
____	3. diverge	c. in current use, it implies "different in good ways"
____	4. gap	d. can be part of a discourse marker, "in _____ to"
____	5. distinguish	e. can occur in the pattern "_____ x from y"
____	6. heterogeneous	f. an undesirable difference between statements, reports,
____	7. diverse	accounts, etc.
____	8. contrast	g. means "go in different directions after having been
____	9. discrepancy	together for a while"
____	10. differ	h. separate; standing apart
		i. like *inequality,* means "difference between values or
		amounts"
		j. a very basic verb meaning "not be the same"; is always
		intransitive

4.8. Usage Practice. Fill each blank in the left column with an item from the right column. Do not use any item more than once.

1. My friend and I did everything together in high school, but   differ

   afterward our lives began to _____.   distinguished

2. The auditors discovered a _____ between   diverge

   the company's financial records and its bank-account statements.   discrepancy

3. The _____ between the salaries of male   disparity

   engineers and female engineers is a serious injustice.   discrete

4. The durian is _____ from other tropical

   fruits by its spiked shell and its strong odor.

5. Inert gases _____ from other gases in that

   they rarely enter into chemical reactions.

6. If a project is too large, you might avoid discouragement by

   breaking it into several smaller, _____ tasks.

4.9. Fitting In. Choose the best word to complete each sentence. Write it in the blank.

> *Example:* Because of the heavy rain, we had to <u>alter</u> our plans. (mutate, transform, alter)

1. Carverville, where almost everyone is of German descent, is one of the least ethnically _____ communities in Ohio. (discrete, heterogeneous, diverse)

2. Latham's designs and Harcourt's followed similar lines in their early years but began to _____ after Latham developed an interest in Japanese architecture. (diverge, distinguish, differ)

3. We have actively sought to make our workforce more _____ _____ by hiring members of minority groups. (diverse, differentiate, divergent)

4. The presence of a carboxyl group (COOH) _____ most organic acids from their inorganic counterparts. (contrasts, differs, differentiates)

5. In the smoke and confusion of battle, the soldiers had trouble _____ _____ friends from enemies. (distinguishing, diverging, differing)

6. If we want to win this election, we'll have to bridge the _____ _____ between liberals and moderates in our party and get them to unite behind us. (contrast, gap, disparity)

7. The researchers figured out the code by breaking large data streams into _____ parts and analyzing each one separately. (discrete, diverse, disparate)

8. Peterson's cost estimate and Van Houten's _____ by only about $1,000. (diverge, differ, differentiate)

9. During the 1970s, it was fashionable for rich people to speak out against social

_____ , but most of them never took any action to correct

it. (disparity, differences, inequality)

10. My favorite teacher, Ms. Howe, was amazing. Somehow, she was able to

appeal to the _____ interests of 25 teenagers at once and

keep us all engaged and entertained. (discrete, disparate, distinguished)

4.10. Combinations and Collocations. Fill in each blank with a word or phrase that fits well with the key vocabulary item. Many answers are possible for most items (except items 1 and 2).

1. The populations of Niles City and Madison differ _____

_____ only a few hundred people, but Madison is a

much busier place.

2. There's a shameful inequality _____

_____ social status among people of various occupations in the village.

3. _____ distinguishes the top

universities from those that are merely adequate.

4. Paintings have to be enjoyed as whole, integrated, visual experiences. It's

wrong to try _____ a work of

art into discrete features.

5. British society is becoming more heterogeneous as a result of _____

_____ .

6. Most Americans can't differentiate _____

_____ from _____ .

7. _____ diverged from those of

my friends as I grew older.

8. Americans and Canadians, though similar in many ways, differ in _____

_____ .

9. The disparity between _____

   and _____ could lead to a

   very dangerous situation.

10. The president claimed that freer international trade would close the gap

    between _____.

🅰🅱 Additional Vocabulary for Chapter 4

The additional words that have come up in the In Context examples in chapter 4 can be found in Appendix 1. (They are underlined when they occur in the In Context sections.) These terms are not fully explained, but you should be able to understand them from the contexts and brief explanations that are given. Do the exercises below to help solidify your understanding of these words.

4.11. Additional Vocabulary 1: Meanings. In each blank, write the letter of the meaning from column B that goes best with each vocabulary item in column A.

Column A

_____ 1. lack
_____ 2. regulation
_____ 3. confiscate
_____ 4. revenue
_____ 5. infrastructure
_____ 6. massive
_____ 7. attend to
_____ 8. portfolio
_____ 9. savvy
_____ 10. distaste
_____ 11. tornado
_____ 12. innocent

Column B

a. a very violent, twisting windstorm
b. take (something) away
c. very large
d. knowledge or ability to understand
e. not guilty
f. a situation in which you don't have enough of something
g. a dislike; a tendency to not want something
h. take care of
i. rule
j. money that you take in
k. a group of investments
l. basic services, like roads or water supply

4.12. Additional Vocabulary 2: Fitting into Sentences. Fill each blank with one of the additional vocabulary items from the list below. You may have to change the form of an item to fit the grammar of the sentence. Do not use any item more than once. Some items will not be used at all.

auditor	innocent	parent company
boom	negotiator	puzzling
immoral	obstacle	regulation
income	otherwise	revolution

1. Even though drinking alcohol, like whiskey or vodka, is now legal, many

    people still consider it _____.

2. Metrofood, a huge corporation, is the _____ of

    several smaller firms like Eatwell, Inc., and AspenStores.

3. They got into financial trouble because their expenses exceeded their

   _____ .

4. The _____ in Internet sales hurt traditional

   "brick-and-mortar" retail stores.

5. Keep your password secret. _____ , people

   could read your e-mail without your permission.

6. Many twentieth-century _____ were religious,

   with secular governments falling to popular movements led by priests or

   mullahs.

7. It took three years for Jones to prove that he was _____

   _____ of the murder.

8. The lack of growth in the industry is _____ .

   I have no idea why things have been so slow.

9. The tax authorities sent a(n) _____ to examine

   his records.

10. Lack of communication is the biggest _____ in

    any marriage, so the best advice is "Talk to each other."

◫ Writing Projects

4.13. Writing Projects. The following are some suggestions for writing projects that will allow you to use the key vocabulary and some of the additional vocabulary. Each of the topics could be lightly covered in an essay of 500–600 words or more thoroughly in a paper of 1,500–2,000 words. To write information-packed longer papers (especially in writing about item 2) you should do some research in the library and/or on the Internet. *Note:* It may feel more natural in your essay for you to discuss similarities as well as differences. Please feel free to do so. (For help with vocabulary about similarities, see chap. 3.)

1. Think about your life 10 years ago and your life now. Use the key vocabulary to describe some of the differences. Consider such things as money, time, possessions, abilities, and opportunities.

2. Choose one of the following situations in which contrasts exist. Do some research to gather facts about specific differences, organize your facts, and write an essay according to specific directions from your teacher. *Hint:* The thesis (or main idea) of your essay should not be that there are differences between/among the elements you're writing about. It's obvious that there are differences. A better thesis would be that the differences are significant in some way, that they indicate something that's not immediately obvious about the situation, or that the differences imply something about the future.

    (a) The differences between one group of nations and another group. Some groups you might want to contrast: the members of NATO (North Atlantic Treaty Organization) and the members of the OAU (Organization for African Unity); the members of ASEAN (Association of Southeast Asian Nations) and the European Union; nations with a strong Confucian heritage and nations with a strong Christian heritage; etc. Please feel free to choose different groupings to contrast.

    (b) The natural environment of Earth as a whole (or some smaller region) at two points in history that you'd like to write about. You can consider any or all factors in the environment—temperatures, rainfall patterns, areas of forest or desert, cleanliness of the air and water, populations of animals, etc. For example, many interesting contrasts could be drawn between the climate of Europe now and the climate of Europe during the 800s (often called the Age of the Vikings), when a period of warm weather significantly affected agriculture, population movements, and cultural development.

Chapter 5   **Changes, Increases, Decreases**

This vocabulary may be useful when:
You want to say exactly how something has changed—very much or not very much, in a good or bad way, etc.

Key Vocabulary			
Group 1	**Group 2**	**Group 3**	**Group 4**
alter	transform	raise	reduce
modify	redesign	rise	diminish
transition	restructure	accelerate	contract
		expand	decline

❖ Exploring the Vocabulary

Group 1. In general (for most kinds of change)

alter

Form	Common Related Forms
Verb (transitive/intransitive)	*alteration* (noun; uncountable when it means "the process of altering"; countable when it means "changes" or "occasions when changes are made")

In Context 1

The burning of <u>fossil fuels</u> has altered Earth's <u>atmosphere</u> more than any other human activity.

In Context 2

The <u>feminist</u> writer Valerie Grissom altered her approach after recognizing that her <u>militant</u> statements were inspiring violence against innocent males.

In Other Words

The air around the Earth has been changed more by the burning of fossil fuels (oil, coal, etc.) than by anything else people do.

In Other Words

Valerie Grissom was a feminist writer (a writer who emphasizes the interests of women). She used to say it was okay to use force in making things better for women, but she changed the way she expressed her ideas because she saw that her writing was encouraging women to attack men who had done nothing wrong.

USAGE CLUES:

- Means "to change some aspect of a thing without changing its basic nature"
- Some common objects: plans, approaches, styles, ideas, statements, written things, schedules, routines, procedures, environments, arrangements, situations
- An adverb or adjective may say how big the change is (e.g., "alter something *slightly*," "a *minor* alteration," "*radically* alters").
- Works well for changes to microscopic organisms (e.g., "altered the virus/ bacterium") or for aspects of larger living things (e.g., "altered the rabbit's immune system") but not usually for changes to large living things as a whole (e.g., it would look strange if you wrote "The years at college altered Bob"; use "changed Bob" instead)
- When *alter* is intransitive, its subject is the thing that changes—not the agent that causes the change (e.g., "His beliefs altered over the course of several years").
- Some common expressions with *alter*

    doesn't alter the fact that—You may be the governor's son, but *that doesn't alter the fact that* you need a license to drive in this state (meaning "It doesn't matter that you're an important person's son. You still need a license")

    mood altering—Even drugs as mild as caffeine can be mood altering (meaning "can change the way you feel")

- When the noun *alteration* means "the process of altering," it might be followed by an *of* phrase (e.g., "Neurotransmitters play a crucial role in the alteration of one's moods").
- When *alteration* means "a change," it might be followed by a *to* or *in* phrase (e.g., "A few alterations to/in the committee's membership should ensure that our proposal gets approved").

 To Help You Remember:

Alter comes from the Latin word for "other." If you alter something, you give it an*other* appearance or aspect.

modify

Form	Common Related Forms
Verb (transitive)	*modification* (noun; countable when it means "a change" or "an occasion for making changes"; uncountable when it means "the process of making changes")

In Context 1

It is possible to modify an ordinary car engine so it <u>runs</u> smoothly <u>on</u> ethanol.

In Other Words

It is possible to make some relatively small changes to a car engine so it operates well by burning ethanol (C_2H_6O—a kind of alcohol that can be made from corn [maize]).

In Context 2

If you want to speak about sex to this audience, you'll have to modify your approach to avoid offending them.

In Other Words

If you want to speak about sex to this group, you'll have to make a few changes in how you do it, so you don't make them angry or uncomfortable.

USAGE CLUES:

- The basic meaning is "to make a small (or moderate) change, usually to solve some problem."
- Usually indicates a positive or neutral opinion about the change. Don't use it if you want to show a negative opinion of the change.
- Some common objects: machines, systems, plans, ideas, statements, routines, procedures, behavior
- The purpose for modifying something might be stated in a clause beginning with *so* (see In Context 1) or in a verbal phrase beginning with *to* (see In Context 2) or *in order to*.
- If the noun form *modification* means "the process of modifying," it might be followed by an *of* phrase + the thing being modified (e.g., "The modification of the plan took a long time"). If *modification* means "a change," use a *to* phrase + the thing being modified (e.g., "We made a few modifications to our schedule").

transition

Form	Common Related Forms
Noun (countable/uncountable)	*transitional* (adjective) NOT in this meaning: *transit*

In Context 1

In the 1960s, the American economy underwent a transition from an industrial system to an information-based system.

In Other Words

In the 1960s, the American economy changed from one that mostly made products to one that mostly processed information.

In Context 2

Many of the unemployed Americans in the survey portrayed themselves as persons in transition.

In Other Words

Many of the jobless Americans who answered the researchers' questions described themselves as being in the process of changing from one condition to another.

USAGE CLUES:

- Emphasizes that the change is taking a long time—and is not yet complete
- Is often followed by a *from . . . to* prepositional structure (see In Context 1)
- You *make* or *undergo* a transition (see In Context 1).
- Often occurs in a set phrase, *in transition* (see In Context 2). This phrase
    Comes directly after its head noun ("persons *in transition*") or after a linking verb—almost always *be* ("the people were *in transition*")
    Does not contain *the* or *a*. Used like this, it doesn't mention the exact nature of the change (see In Context 2). If you change this phrase to "in *the* transition," you must be sure to make clear exactly which transition you mean.

As They Say

The more things change, the more they remain the same.

Things may seem very different, but, at a deeper level, they are much the same as they have been for a long time.

This phrase is a rough English translation of a phrase from the French playwright Alphonse Karr: "Plus ça change, plus c'est la même chose." This French phrase—or the first part of it—often appears in English conversation.

For example:

A: I hear the government wants to start taxing people for using the Internet.

B: Plus ça change . . .

Speaker B means that, even though a somewhat new technology is involved, the government is doing an old, familiar thing—imposing a tax.

Consolidation Exercises: Group 1

5.1. Prepositions. Fill each blank with the best of the following prepositions: *by, for, from, in, to, with.* Some prepositions will be used more than once; others will not be used at all.

1. We had to make a few slight modifications _____ the design of the container.

2. The transition _____ a relatively carefree, childless lifestyle _____ responsible parenthood is difficult for many couples.

3. The boss maintained very tight control over his employees. He had to approve even the smallest alteration _____ their work schedules.

4. We had to modify our proposal several times _____ satisfy the committee.

5.2. Rephrasing. Using *alter, modify,* or *transition,* rephrase each of the following passages (write it in other words). You may change the form of the item you use to fit the grammar of what you write. Change the words of the original passage as much as necessary but don't change the meaning.

1. Cotton farming near the Aral Sea in Kazakhstan has used up a lot of water that would otherwise have gone to the sea. Because of this, the Aral Sea is now much smaller than it was in 1970.

2. The economies of some European countries are changing. The governments of these countries used to own all or most of the factories and service companies. Slowly, these government-owned businesses are being sold to private investors.

3. Some analysts say that birth-control pills, which became widely available in the 1960s, helped change the role of women in American society.

4. After Hong Kong became the world's hottest market for cellular phones, Globe-Vest Telecommunications, Inc., had to make some changes to its marketing plan.

5. Over many years, the majority of North Americans have slowly come to believe that preserving the natural environment is sometimes more important than promoting economic growth.

Group 2. Large or basic changes

transform

Form	Common Related Forms
Verb (transitive)	*transformation* (noun; uncountable when it means "the process of making big changes to something"; countable when it means "a change" or "an occasion when something is greatly changed") *transformable* (adjective meaning "able to be greatly changed") *transformative* (adjective meaning "causing great change")

In Context 1

The printing press transformed Flanders from an idea-poor, Church-<u>dominated</u> region into a haven for freethinkers.

In Other Words

The printing press (a machine that makes many copies of written material by pressing ink onto paper) changed Flanders in very deep and basic ways. Flanders used to be controlled by the church, but it became a place where people felt they could think freely.

In Context 2

Shamsuddin was transformed by his journey to the holy cities.

In Other Words

Traveling to the holy cities changed Shamsuddin in deep and important ways.

USAGE CLUES:

- Can be followed by a *from . . . into* structure (see In Context 1). The *into* could be replaced by *to*.
- Should have an object, even if something causes a change to itself (e.g., China transformed *itself* in the 1980s and 1990s")
- A person or a thing can *undergo* or *experience* or *go through* a transformation (e.g., Last year she made the *transformation* from college to student to working woman").
- Transformations can *take place* or *occur.*
- *BE CAREFUL:* The noun *transformer* usually means "a device that changes electrical current"—NOT usually "something or someone that causes great change." To express this meaning, use a phrase like *factor in* or *cause of* plus the noun *transformation* (e.g., "The main *factor in* the transformation of social attitudes toward smoking was . . .").

redesign

Form	Common Related Forms
Verb (transitive)	*redesign* (noun, uncountable)

In Context 1

<u>Advocates</u> of Japanese-style management have urged many American businesses to redesign themselves to promote <u>consensus</u> among workers.

In Context 2

It would cost many millions of dollars to redesign the aircraft to operate with a smaller, more <u>fuel-efficient</u> engine.

In Other Words

People who like the way Japanese businesses are managed have encouraged many American companies to change their basic character so that workers can more easily reach agreement about how to operate.

In Other Words

It would cost several million dollars to change the basic structure of the airplane so that it could have a smaller engine that uses less fuel.

USAGE CLUES:

- Redesigning always involves thought and planning. It usually happens because an earlier plan or structure no longer fits present circumstances.
- Some common objects: machines, systems, organizations
- As a noun to mean "the process of making a basic change" you can use either *redesign* (most commonly in a definite noun phrase, often including *of:* "the redesign of the marketing system") or *redesigning* (when you want to make an indefinite noun phrase: "redesigning the marketing system").

restructure

Form	Common Related Forms
Verb (transitive)	*restructuring* (noun, uncountable)

In Context 1

Foreign banks agreed to restructure Kalistan's <u>debt</u> because of the country's severe economic problems.

In Other Words

Banks from other countries agreed to set up a new system for Kalistan to pay back the money it owed them.

In Context 2

Restructuring the CIA was difficult because of resistance from agency <u>veterans</u>.

In Other Words

Making big changes to the basic structure of the CIA was difficult because people who had worked there for a long time didn't want the changes to be made.

USAGE CLUES:

- Like redesigning, restructuring always involves thought and planning.
- Some things you can restructure: systems, schedules, and companies
- You cannot restructure machines. (That's a difference between *redesign* and *restructure.*)

- Sometimes, *restructure* can appear without an object. In that case it means "restructure itself/themselves" (e.g., "The advertising company knew it would have to restructure to handle its new clients").
- A phrase common in discussions of finance is *restructure* [someone's] *debt.* This means "set a new schedule for someone to pay back money that is owed."

Consolidation Exercises: Group 2

5.3. Meanings and Connections. Next to each statement, write *transform, redesign,* or *restructure*—whichever best fits the description.

_____ a. is similar in meaning to *redesign* but can't be used

for machines

_____ b. is often followed by a *from . . . into* structure

_____ and _____ c. These two words

both imply thought and planning

5.4. Collocations. Fill each blank with a word or phrase that goes well with the key vocabulary item. There are several possible answers to numbers 1 and 3. *Hint:* Look at the Usage Clues and consider some of the additional vocabulary introduced in this section.

1. In the movie *My Fair Lady,* a professor tries to change a rough young woman

   into a cultured lady, but the professor _____ a

   great personal transformation as well.

2. In the presence of water, the seeds are quickly transformed _____

   _____ dry granules _____ tender,

   light-green sprouts.

3. The increased use of computers for trading shares in companies made it

   necessary to redesign the nation's _____.

4. Severe economic problems made it difficult for many companies to pay back what they had borrowed from TransOcean Bank. The bank had little choice but to restructure these companies' _____ .

5.5. Rephrasing. Using some form of *transform, redesign,* or *restructure,* rephrase each of the following passages (write it in other words). You may change the form of the item to fit the grammar of what you write. Change the words of the original passage as much as necessary but don't change the meaning.

1. The Hanscomb company's CD players worked very well, but their appearance was a bit old fashioned. It was clear that the Hanscomb people would have to make some changes if they wanted to improve sales.

2. The management consultant saw a big organizational problem at Growtech, Inc. Managers were not giving talented people enough freedom to act on their own ideas. The consultant recommended that the company change in ways that would remove some of the restrictions on creative people.

3. Some governments believe they can increase national productivity by simply putting "creative thinking" modules into their national school programs. This is wrongheaded and simplistic. If you want creative thinkers, you need a social system that encourages independence and doesn't punish people for peacefully saying what they think.

4. Years of chaos brought about by famine and civil war have changed the Republic of Abaca completely. The roads, railroads, water supply, and electricity grid used to be of world-class quality, but those have been mostly destroyed. The country now has a very primitive way of life.

5. Once someone is elected to Congress, he or she soon finds that there is little time or incentive to actually think about passing laws. The next election will be in four years, and the wise congressperson immediately starts preparing for it. His or her main job soon becomes getting reelected. This system of frequent reelections blocks our nation's progress and must be changed.

Group 3. Increasing

raise

Form	Common Related Forms
Verb (transitive)	*raise* (noun, countable; usable only to mean "an increase in pay at your job")

In Context 1

The new anticancer drug raised the company's profits by 20 percent this year.

In Other Words

The new drug to fight cancer caused the company's profits this year to be 20 percent higher than last year's profits.

In Context 2

Grover University raised its admission standards and began interviewing prospective students more carefully.

In Other Words

Grover University decided that people who wanted to enter the university had to show a higher level of achievement. The university also became more careful in its conversations with people who wanted to enter.

USAGE CLUES:

- Is always transitive, with both a subject and an object. If you want to make an intransitive statement use *rise*. (See the entry for *rise* below.)
- The subject can be a person, a group (see In Context 2), a nonliving factor (see In Context 1), a condition, or an event.
- Some common objects: *standard* (see in Context 2), *profile,* amounts, levels, values, scores
- *BE CAREFUL:* In this meaning, the object CANNOT be the word *money,* the word *cash,* or a phrase giving an amount of money (e.g., "$550"). The object can be a word related to money (*fee, income, profits,* etc.), as in In Context 1.
- *BE CAREFUL:* The noun *raise* is usable ONLY to mean "an increase in pay." In other contexts, use the noun *rise* or *increase.*

To Help You Remember:

- The base meaning is "to take something from a low position to a higher one."
- An old word in English, it is related to the English verb *rear,* which also means "raise." You can *rear children* ("raise them," "help them grow up"). A horse can *rear up* by lifting its front legs while standing on its back legs.

rise

Form	Common Related Forms
Verb (intransitive)	*rise* (noun, countable)

In Context 1

The danger of war has risen since last year's nuclear-missile tests.

In Other Words

The chance that a war might break out is greater than it was last year, when someone tested missiles that had nuclear explosives attached to them.

In Context 2

The department's income from speaking fees rose by about 15% per year in the 1990s.

In Other Words

In the 1990s, the amount of money the department got when its members spoke to various groups was about 15% higher each year than it was the year before.

USAGE CLUES:

- The simple past form is *rose;* the past participle is *risen.*
- Some common subjects: *incidence (of X), temperature, water* (in a river, lake, or sea), *tide,* amounts, levels, values, standards, emotions
- Carries an image of a level getting higher, so it works best with subjects that are either like a fluid (e.g., emotions, amounts of money) or like a line that defines a level (e.g., standards)
- Often followed by a phrase
   beginning with *by,* to show how large the increase has been (see In Context 2)
   beginning with *to,* to show a point that something is moving toward
- The noun *rise* is often followed by an *in* phrase that names what is increasing (e.g., "a large rise in popular opposition").

To Help You Remember:

Rise comes from the same origins as the verb *raise*. To remember that *rise* is the *in*transitive one, you might remember that it's shorter than *raise*. *Raise* (the longer word) needs two noun phrases—both a subject and an object. *Rise* (the shorter word) works with only one noun phrase—the subject.

accelerate

Form	Common Related Forms
Verb (transitive/intransitive)	*acceleration* (noun meaning "the process of going faster," uncountable) *accelerator* (noun meaning "something that causes an increase in speed," usually, a pedal in a car, countable) *accelerant* (noun meaning "something that speeds up a process," often, "a chemical that makes a fire spread faster," countable) *accelerated* (verbal adjective)

In Context 1

The race to outline the human <u>genome</u> accelerated after private companies claimed to be near success.

In Other Words

People began working faster to chart the entire sequence of human genes after private companies said they were almost ready to complete the task.

In Context 2

Oxygen and sunshine accelerate the deterioration of the plastic.

In Other Words

Oxygen and sunshine make the plastic weaken and fall apart faster.

USAGE CLUES:

- Always refers to an increase in speed or in a rate of progress
- Some common subjects of the intransitive form—and common objects of the transitive form: the terms *rate, pace, development, growth,* phrases for processes or other things that can have speed (e.g., *race,* In Context 1)
- For the transitive form, some common subjects: forces, conditions, or participants in a process

- The verbal adjective *accelerated* is often used to mean "faster than usual" (e.g., "the economy's accelerated growth during spring and summer").
- *BE CAREFUL:* Processes can accelerate but not the things that are part of the process. For example, prices cannot accelerate, but *increases* in prices CAN accelerate (and so can decreases) because increasing and decreasing are processes.

expand

Form	Common Related Forms
Verb (transitive/intransitive)	*expansion* (noun, uncountable) *expansive* (adjective meaning "broad or stretching for a long distance") *expandable* (adjective meaning "able to be made larger") *expanded* (verbal adjective meaning "larger than it used to be")

In Context 1

In some thermometers, mercury expands as it heats up.

In Other Words

In some thermometers, mercury (Hg) gains volume as it gets warmer.

In Context 2

The research team expanded their scope to include subjects from a wider geographic area.

In Other Words

The research team changed their research plan so it would look into a wider range of things—specifically so it would include information from people from more places.

USAGE CLUES:

- The base meaning is "increase in size by going out in several directions at once."
- In technical contexts (see In Context 1), it is common to describe an increase in volume—which happens when a material (especially a fluid) is exposed to higher temperatures or lower pressures.

- The subject of the intransitive form—AND the object of the transitive—is likely to be *influence, economy, scope, range;* words for areas, volumes, business or trade, programs, efforts, or forces.
- The subject of the transitive form is likely to be a person, a group, or an organization.
- However, the subject of the intransitive form should not normally be a person or another living thing.
- The verbal adjective (*expanded*) is often used to mean simply "larger or longer than usual" (e.g., "Enjoy our expanded summer hours").
- Acts as a sort of opposite to the verb *contract* (see entry for *contract* in the next section of this chapter)

Consolidation Exercises: Group 3

5.6. Collocations. Fill each blank with a word or phrase that goes well with the key vocabulary item. There are several possible answers to numbers 3 and 4. *Hint:* Look at the Usage Clues and consider some of the additional vocabulary introduced in this section.

1. The average test score has risen _____ several points over the past three years.

2. Airline pilots went on strike, demanding a raise in _____ _____.

3. The company decided to expand its _____ in order to reach more potential customers.

4. The _____ of social change has accelerated because of television, the Internet, and other visual media.

5.7. Rephrasing. Use some form of *raise, rise, accelerate,* or *expand* to rephrase each of the following passages (write it in other words). You may change the form of the item to fit the grammar of what you write. Change the words of the original passage as much as necessary but don't change the meaning.

1. Because Greek colonists settled in faraway places like Syracuse, on Sicily, the use of the Greek language reached far beyond what we normally think of as the Greek islands.

2. After several years of being relatively rare in developed societies, tuberculosis (a serious disease of the lungs) began spreading faster in Europe and North America.

3. As the ice caps at the poles of the Earth melt, the level of the oceans throughout the world gets higher.

4. The Costa Rican government spent a lot of money on basic improvements to the country's infrastructure, and this caused the standard of living in Costa Rica to become one of the highest in the region.

Group 4. Decreasing

reduce

Form	Common Related Forms
Verb (transitive)	*reduction* (noun, countable when it means "a lowering" or "an occasion when something gets lowered"; uncountable when it means "the process of lowering") *reduced* (verbal adjective)

In Context 1

The new regulations helped reduce the nation's <u>dependence</u> on foreign oil.

In Other Words

The new rules helped the country bring down its need for oil from other countries.

In Context 2

The drug Blastophene reduces the flow of blood to the brain by about 17%, which can lead to confusion and <u>fatigue</u>.

In Other Words

If someone takes the drug Blastophene, the flow of blood to his or her brain will be about 17% less than normal. This can make the person feel confused and very tired.

USAGE CLUES:

- Some common subjects: humans, organizations, laws, participants in (or parts of) processes
- Some common objects: weight, dependence, conditions, feelings, actions, amounts of time or money, abilities
- Sometimes followed by a *by* phrase to show how much less or how much smaller something has become (see In Context 2)
- The noun *reduction* is often followed by an *in* phrase to name the thing that becomes smaller (e.g., "a reduction in the nation's dependence on foreign oil").
- The verbal adjective *reduced* is often used to mean "less than (or smaller than) usual."

As They Say

> *If it ain't broke, don't fix it.*

Don't make unnecessary changes to things. If you do, you might damage something that is working perfectly well.

This is very informal, much more common in speech than in writing. (Notice the "incorrect" forms of words.) It works very well in informal office conversations, when you think a change might be unwise.

For example:

A: Maybe we ought to think about redesigning the T-31 and making it a bit smaller.
B: What for? It's selling well as it is. If it ain't broke, don't fix it.

diminish

Form	Common Related Forms
Verb (transitive/intransitive)	*diminished* (verbal adjective) *diminution* (noun, uncountable) *diminutive* (adjective meaning "very small")

In Context 1

The threat of rebel attacks diminished after the rainy season began.

In Context 2

A <u>financial</u> <u>scandal</u> diminished the president's <u>influence</u> in Congress.

In Other Words

After the rainy season began, it became less likely that the rebels would attack.

In Other Words

The president had less ability to affect the activities of Congress because he was connected to some widely talked-about dishonest activity involving money.

USAGE CLUES:

- Indicates a decrease in strength, value, or importance
- Especially as a transitive verb, it works very well in contexts where something/someone falls into a weaker position (see In Context 1) or a lower status.
- Some common subjects of the intransitive form—and common objects of the transitive form: *threat, danger, influence, strength,* conditions, feelings, abilities, other things that can have strength or intensity
- A system or an organization is NOT usually the subject of the intransitive verb, although it could be the object of the transitive verb.
- Often occurs in the passive, commonly with an adverb of degree (*greatly, slightly,* etc.) between *be* and *diminished.* (e.g., "His energy was greatly diminished by the illness")

contract

Form	Common Related Forms
Verb (intransitive)	*contraction* (noun; uncountable when it means "the process of contracting"; countable when it means "occasions when something gets smaller") NOT in this meaning: *contract* (noun), *contractual* (adjective)

In Context 1

The economy contracted by about 4% in the first half of 1973.

In Context 2

The cold weather caused the rubber seals to contract, and a leak developed.

In Other Words

Halfway through 1973, the level of economic activity was about 4% less than it had been at the start of the year.

In Other Words

Because of the cold weather the rubber seals (parts that fit tightly into the opening between sections of a machine) became smaller. This caused an opening through which fluids could get out.

USAGE CLUES:

- The base meaning is "getting smaller by moving toward a center from several directions at once."
- Something can contract quickly or slowly, but the process usually occurs because of normal or natural causes—not as the result of a disaster.
- Acts as something of an opposite to *expand*
- May appear with *expand* as part of a pair (e.g., "the economy expands and contracts"), especially in contexts about regular cycles in which things get larger, then smaller, then larger again
- Unlike *expand, contract* is always intransitive.
- In technical contexts (see In Context 2), often describes what happens when a material (especially a fluid) is exposed to lower temperatures or higher pressures
- Common subjects: physical materials, parts of bodies or of machines, volumes, business or trade, or fields of force

 To Help You Remember:

Comes from Latin roots meaning "pull together." When something contracts, it pulls itself together toward its center.

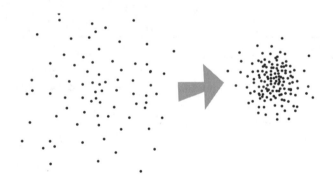

decline

Form	Common Related Forms
Verb (intransitive)	*decline* (noun, countable)

In Context 1

Our research budget has declined by more than 20% in the past two years.

In Context 2

Eventually, Vargas's <u>eyesight</u> declined to the point where he couldn't read a newspaper.

In Other Words

The amount of money we are given to do research has gone down by more than 20% in the past two years.

In Other Words

Over time, Vargas's ability to see became so weak that he couldn't read a newspaper.

USAGE CLUES:

- Some common subjects: systems, amounts, organizations, conditions, abilities, situations
- Is sometimes followed by a *by* phrase to show how much something has weakened or decreased (see In Context 1)
- Might also be followed by a phrase to show a point or situation that lies at the end of the decline. This phrase can begin with a connector like *so far that . . .* or *to the point where . . .* (see In Context 2).
- The noun *decline* often appears in a set adjective phrase—*in decline*—that always comes after the noun it modifies (e.g., "Rome was already an empire in decline").

 To Help You Remember:

Comes from Latin roots meaning "slant or slope downward." Imagine a hill. If you are on top of the hill, the sides of the hill slant downward from where you stand. (In fact, in older or extremely formal English, a downward-sloping hillside would be called "a decline.") Something that declines "goes downhill."

⬚ Consolidation Exercises: Group 4

5.8. Collocations. Fill each blank with a word or phrase that goes well with the key vocabulary item. There are several possible answers to items 1, 2, and 4. *Hint:* Look at the Usage Clues and consider some of the additional vocabulary introduced in this section.

1. The car's sales in Europe declined _____ the manufacturer could no longer afford to keep a sales staff there.

2. America's influence in the region was _____ diminished after the State Department closed most embassy libraries and replaced them with "commercial resource centers."

3. The veins in the human body _____ and contract as blood from the heart travels through the circulatory system.

4. The first people to buy a new electronic device almost always pay a ridiculously high price for it. Technological improvements eventually reduce _____ _____ of electronic goods—even very sophisticated ones.

5. Once America's national game, professional baseball has suffered from too much money and too many scandals. It's now a sport _____ _____ decline.

6. A small reduction _____ the amount of fat you eat can have huge benefits for your health.

5.9. Rephrasing. Using a form of *reduce, diminish, contract, or decline*, rephrase each of the following passages (write it in other words). You may change the form of the item you use to fit the grammar of what you write. Change the words of the original passage as much as necessary but don't change the meaning.

1. The mining company originally thought there were large amounts of gold in the area, but some negative laboratory reports forced them to dramatically lower their estimates.

2. Many middle-class Americans became disgusted with the welfare system (a system for giving food or money to very poor people) and argued that far fewer benefits should be given out through this system.

3. After various industries, such as steelmaking and chemical manufacturing, moved into the area, pollution became very bad. The natural beauty of the region suffered greatly as forests were choked and marshes were poisoned.

4. After Jameson developed a drinking problem, the quality of his writing became worse, and his influence among New York publishers weakened.

5. After many countries stopped burning coal to generate electricity, the market for coal became a lot smaller than it used to be.

👁 Comprehensive Review Exercises

5.10. Matching. Next to each item in the left column, write the letter of the best meaning from the right column. Do not use any letter more than once.

____ 1. raise	a. change the basic arrangement or structure of something
____ 2. alter	b. get worse or weaker, as if "going downhill"
____ 3. accelerate	c. make smaller or less; always transitive
____ 4. redesign	d. get larger by moving out in several directions at once
____ 5. contract	e. the process of moving from one condition to another
____ 6. expand	f. make a new plan for something
____ 7. rise	g. put something in a higher position; always transitive
____ 8. transition	h. make some changes, usually to correct a problem or adjust to new conditions
____ 9. diminish	i. increase in speed or rate
____ 10. restructure	j. change something so much that it no longer looks the same
____ 11. transform	k. change an aspect of something, without changing its basic nature; from a Latin root meaning "other"
____ 12. reduce	l. go to a higher position; always intransitive
____ 13. decline	m. get smaller by shrinking back toward a center
____ 14. modify	n. make or get smaller or weaker; often implies a loss of status

5.11. Usage Practice. Choose the best item from the right column to fill each blank in the left column. Write the item in the blank. Do not use any item more than once.

1. The rate of change will _____.   contracts

2. Gases _____ when heated.   redesign

3. This refrigerator won't appeal to Japanese buyers. We'll have to   transition

     totally _____ it.   accelerate

4. My _____ to a new job was difficult.   modify

5. If the economy _____, there'll be a depression.   expand

6. We don't need a new system. We can just _____

     the old one.

5.12. Fitting In. Choose the best word or phrase to complete each sentence. Write it in the blank.

> *Example:* Because of the heavy rain, we had to <u>alter</u> our plans. (reduce, transform, alter)

1. Following a series of crashes, the Stavanger Aircraft Company was forced to completely _____ the tail section of its N474 transport plane. (alter, redesign, restructure)

2. After years of drought and mismanagement, the nation's agricultural base had _____ to the point where only a miracle could revive it. (reduced, diminished, declined)

3. By _____, the company was able to halve its payroll costs without cutting back on its operations. (restructuring, being in transition, diminishing)

4. This schedule could work, but the break periods are too short. You should _____ those to give people a bit of rest. (expand, raise, accelerate)

5. Some people believe that the Internet suddenly appeared in the mid-1990s. In fact, it took more than 20 years for the Net to _____ _____ from obscurity and become a far-reaching commercial phenomenon. (raise, rise, redesign)

6. The Millennium Watchfulness Brotherhood was a group of people who expected the world's computer systems to collapse in the year 2000, leading to a complete social _____. Sophisticated civilizations would be _____ to primitive, constantly warring tribes of hunter-gatherers. (transformation, transition, contraction)/(reduced, modified, expanded)

7. Health care costs for the average American _____ _____ as the population aged and the demand for medical services grew. (accelerated, raised, rose)

8. The plant was sold to a Belgian firm, whose managers took several months to become familiar with the operation. It was then, as a factory _____ _____ from local to foreign management, that Community Metalworks faced its greatest challenge. (in decline, in reduction, in transition)

9. We have achieved enormous growth during the last ten years without _____ _____ our basic approach to business: "Every customer is special." (diminishing, altering, redesigning)

5.13. Combinations and Collocations. Fill in the blank with a word or phrase that fits well with the key vocabulary item. Many answers are possible in all items except 1 and 4.

1. By making a few modifications _____ _____ the treaty, the negotiators were able to satisfy both sides and end the fighting.

2. About five years ago, the nation _____ _____ an economic transformation as its banking system was completely restructured.

3. When _____ doesn't receive much water—either from rain or irrigation—it contracts; cracks then appear.

4. Last year was a good one for the fiber-optics industry, with sales of new cable rising _____ more than 18%.

5. Management consultants, eager to seem useful, often urge senior executives to redesign _____ that are basically sound and healthy. Wise executives will remember the useful adage: "If it ain't broke, don't fix it."

6. Bernard Gordon's latest book complains that _____ _____ has diminished America's reputation in Asia, whose people now consider the U.S. a passive society addicted to cheap entertainment.

7. _____ accelerated the

   development of the U.S. effort to land humans on the moon.

8. After a few troublemakers were expelled from the school, _____

   _____ declined. An environment that had

   been one of the most dangerous in the entire system became a calm, quiet

   place of study and exploration.

9. A rapid rise _____ is often an

   indicator that a volcano is about to erupt.

10. By _____ a few alterations

    _____ your present computer

    network, you could process about twice as many orders each day.

Additional Vocabulary for Chapter 5

The additional words and phrases that have come up in the In Context examples in chapter 5 can be found in Appendix 1. (They are underlined when they occur in the In Context sections.) These terms are not fully explained, but you should be able to understand them from the contexts and brief explanations that are given. Do the exercises below to help solidify your understanding of these words and phrases.

5.14. Additional Vocabulary 1: Meanings. In each blank, write the letter of the meaning from column B that goes best with each vocabulary item in column A.

Column A
_____ 1. eyesight
_____ 2. militant
_____ 3. seal
_____ 4. atmosphere
_____ 5. fatigue
_____ 6. prospective
_____ 7. standard
_____ 8. feminist
_____ 9. financial
_____ 10. genome
_____ 11. influence
_____ 12. debt

Column B
a. the level at which something is considered good enough
b. possible
c. related to money
d. willing to use force or violence to achieve one's goals
e. one or several layers of gas around a planet
f. the ability to see
g. a part (of a machine or structure) that keeps gases or liquids from getting through
h. the ability to get people to do what you want
i. money (or something else) that should be paid or given to someone else
j. extreme tiredness
k. the overall pattern of genes that a species has
l. especially concerned with the interests and rights of women

5.15. Additional Vocabulary 2: Fitting into Sentences. Fill each blank with one of the additional vocabulary items from the list below. You may have to change the form of the item to fit the grammar of the sentence. Do not use any item more than once. Some items will not be used at all.

advocate   feminist   run on
consensus   fossil fuels   scandal
dependence   influence   standard
dominate   leak   veteran
              militant

1. Winning nearly every major tournament, Willie Borges _____

_____ the game of tennis during the 1990s.

2. The walls became wet and began to deteriorate because of a(n) _____

_____ in the roof.

3. News organizations like to report on sexual or financial _____

_____ in government, because such stories are very dramatic.

4. The East Minnesota Coalition for the Homeless _____

_____ using tax money to build more shelters for people who might

otherwise freeze to death while sleeping on the streets.

5. The new therapy helps people stop smoking by reducing their bodies'

_____ on nicotine, an addictive chemical in

cigarette smoke.

6. Modern management theories hold that an executive's ability to _____

_____ an organization's policies and practices depends on

an ability to achieve _____ among the affected

employees.

7. I would buy gas mixed with alcohol if I could be sure my car's engine would

_____ that kind of fuel even during cold weather.

8. Even though young, aggressive traders were important to the firm's success,

each work team needed a few _____ with

enough experience to see trouble coming and figure out ways of avoiding it.

▌▌ Writing Projects

5.16. Writing Projects. The following are some suggestions for writing projects that will allow you to use the key vocabulary and some of the additional vocabulary. Each of the topics could be lightly covered in an essay of 500–600 words or more thoroughly in a paper of 1,500–2,000 words. To write information-packed longer papers you should do some research in the library and/or on the Internet.

1. Some wildlife photographers (people who take pictures of animals in their natural surroundings) have been accused of "cheating" in several ways:

   cruelly bothering animals to get interesting shots

   artificially creating dramatic pictures by using captive animals, not truly wild ones

   using computers to change photographs in ways that misrepresent the original event

   Express your opinion about some aspect of this issue. For example:

   Do you think wildlife photographers have the right to use these techniques in order to get better shots or to make existing shots look more interesting?

   Should wildlife photographers be more strictly controlled in order to protect animals?

2. The Earth's atmosphere is getting warmer. This warming has been attributed to many causes. Some people suggest natural causes, such as the greenhouse effect (the trapping of heat by atmospheric gases) and a natural cycle of cool and warm periods. Others believe that this is the result of the activities of humans. Still others say that, whatever the cause, global warming is not really a bad thing. Express your opinion about some aspect of this issue. For example:

   Is global warming necessarily a bad thing?

   What do you think is/are the most important factor(s) in global warming?

   If global warming is undesirable, what can be done to stop it or slow it down?

Chapter 6 Links, Correlations, Happening Together

This vocabulary may be useful when:

Two or more things are found together—but one doesn't necessarily cause the other. Research commonly discovers such correlations.

Key Vocabulary

Group 1	Group 2	Group 3
link	accompany	characteristic of
correlation	go along with	associated with

Group 4		Group 5
in conjunction with		imply
to the degree that		infer

❖ Exploring the Vocabulary

Group 1. Nouns that mean "a relationship in which two things go together"

link

Form	Common Related Forms
Noun (countable)	*linkage* (noun, countable/uncountable)
	link (verb, transitive)

In Context 1

The article reported that researchers have discovered a link between <u>baldness</u> and mathematical ability, although this could be mere <u>coincidence</u>.

In Context 2

It's hard to deny smoking's link with cancer.

In Other Words

According to the article, researchers have found that a bald person (someone who has no hair on part or all of the head) is more likely than other people to be good at mathematics, but this connection could have occurred simply by chance, not for any special reason.

In Other Words

It is very clear that there is a strong connection between smoking and having cancer.

USAGE CLUES:

- The base meaning is "connection." *Link* does NOT mean that one of the connected things causes the other, but in some cases a causal relationship is possible (see In Context 2).
- Works well in contexts of research that finds a pattern of "occurring together"— where you find one thing, you also often find another.
- Often followed by a *between . . . and* structure (see In Context 1) naming both connected things
- The verb *link* is usually in the passive (e.g., "Smoking has been *linked* to cancer").
- You may see *linkage* as a replacement for *link* (e.g., "The *linkage* between smoking and cancer is strong"), but *link* is better because it's shorter.

 To Help You Remember:

A link is one piece of a <u>chain</u>. Using *link* to mean "connection" is a metaphor, suggesting the image of a chain.

correlation

Form	Common Related Forms
Noun (countable)	*correlate* (verb, transitive/intransitive) *correlate* (noun meaning "a thing that usually occurs with another," countable) *correlative* (adjective meaning "related") *correlative* (noun meaning "one thing that is related to another," countable)

In Context 1

Our research showed a strong correlation between home ownership and membership in community-improvement organizations.

In Other Words

Our research showed that people who have bought houses are very likely to join groups that try to make cities or towns better places to live.

In Context 2

Garrity investigated <u>suicide</u>'s close correlation with unemployment.

In Other Words

Garrity tried to find out more about the fact that many people who kill themselves had recently not been able to find jobs.

USAGE CLUES:

- Very often followed by a *between . . . and* structure naming the things that correlate (see In Context 1)
- If one of the connected things is named before the noun *correlation,* a *with* phrase might follow to name the other (see In Context 2).
- There is a technical usage in statistical contexts: a number with a decimal point in it might indicate how frequently two things go together. For example, *a correlation of .50* indicates that two things can be found together in about one-half of all cases.
- In a correlation, the two things not only happen together but probably increase or decrease together. For example, In Context 1 indicates that a rise in home ownership and a rise in membership would occur together; similarly, a fall in home ownership and a fall in membership would occur together.
- The word *correlation* does not actually mean that one thing causes the other, but in many cases, a correlation *could* include a causal relationship (see In Context 2; the unemployment might lead to the suicide).
- Some adjectives that often appear with correlation: *strong, weak, high, low, close, direct*
- The verb *correlate* is usually intransitive and is usually followed by a *with* phrase (e.g., "The weight of a newborn baby correlates strongly with the parents' annual income").
- As a transitive verb, *correlate* means "establish that a connection exists" (e.g., "New measurement techniques helped Dr. Henman correlate unemployment with suicide rates").

Group 2. Verbs that mean "go together with"

accompany

Form	Common Related Forms
Verb (transitive)	*accompanying* (verbal adjective) NOT in this meaning: *accompaniment*

In Context 1

Muscle <u>aches</u> routinely accompany high <u>fevers</u>.

In Other Words

Someone who has a high fever (a body temperature much higher than normal) is also likely to feel some pain in his or her muscles.

In Context 2

<u>Cardiac</u> problems are often accompanied by a general <u>depression</u>, even in patients who are unaware that they have heart problems.

In Other Words

In many cases, a person with a heart problem is likely to feel generally sad and dissatisfied, even if that person doesn't know that he or she has a heart problem.

USAGE CLUES:

- Its "link/correlation" meaning is an extension of its basic meaning—"to go along with, especially as a friend."
- Is very often passive (see In Context 2)
- If one factor is more basic, important, or obvious than the other, it will be the object of the active verb or the subject of the passive (see *fever* and *cardiac problems* in In Context 1 and 2).
- The object of the active verb cannot be a *that* clause. By rephrasing *that* as *the fact that,* you can make an acceptable object (e.g., "Confusion accompanied the fact that telephone lines had been damaged by the storm").
- The adjective *accompanying* is very common (e.g., "a recession and the *accompanying* rise in unemployment").

go along with

Form	Common Related Forms
Two-word verb (intransitive) + preposition	None

In Context 1

Disorientation often goes along with <u>jet lag</u>.

In Other Words

If you have jet lag (a condition in which someone who has traveled a long distance east or west to a different <u>time zone</u> in a short time feels tired and out of touch with local time) you are also likely to feel confused.

In Context 2

Among Americans, an increase in patriotic feeling usually goes along with such occasions as the Fourth of July or a presidential election.

In Other Words

On some occasions like the Fourth of July (a holiday celebrating American independence) and presidential elections, Americans feel more positively about their country than they usually do.

USAGE CLUES:

- The "link/connection" meaning is an extension of the basic meaning—"travel together with (a more important thing)."
- The subject will be a smaller, less basic, or less important thing than the object of the preposition.
- The object of *with* cannot be a *that* clause. By rephrasing *that* as *the fact that*, you can make an acceptable object (e.g., "Confusion went along with the fact that telephone lines had been damaged by the storm").

Consolidation Exercises: Groups 1 and 2

6.1. Collocations. Fill each blank with a word or phrase that goes well with the key vocabulary item. There are several possible answers to items 3 and 4. *Hint:* Look at the Usage Clues and consider some of the additional vocabulary introduced in this section.

    1. There is no solid evidence of a link _____

       _____ microwave radiation and cancer.

2. DeBoer's study confirmed that the presence of spotted beetles shows a high correlation _____ atmospheric humidity.

3. _____ usually go(es) along with the development of heavy industry, such as steelmaking or car production.

4. Strong winds often accompany _____

_____ .

6.2. Rephrasing. Using *link, correlation, accompany,* or *go along with,* rephrase each of the following passages (write it in other words). You may change the form of the item you use to fit the grammar of what you write. Change the words of the original passage as much as necessary but don't change the meaning.

1. Surveys have shown that vegetarians (people who don't eat meat) are likely to vote for liberal candidates in elections for public office.

2. In a recent survey, more than half of the people who said they earned more than $50,000 also said they were members of health clubs.

3. It is very common for outbreaks of diseases to occur during periods of social unrest, such as civil wars or very big changes in government.

4. Cultures in which many people are (or once were) farmers usually have a harvest festival of some kind, in which they celebrate the successful gathering of crops.

5. Men who complain of sudden weakness in their arms and legs are often found to have lower-than-normal levels of the hormone testosterone.

Group 3. Adjective phrases that mean "connected with"

characteristic of

Form	Common Related Forms
Adjective + preposition	*characteristically* (adverb) *characteristic* (noun, countable) *characterize* (verb, transitive) NOT in this meaning: *character* (noun, countable)

In Context 1

The study found that high telephone rates are characteristic of low-<u>wage</u> economies.

In Other Words

The study found that where workers do not earn very much money, prices for using telephones are high.

In Context 2

Efficiency in the ocean-shipping industry has increased because of the larger docks characteristic of modern port facilities.

In Other Words

The business of shipping things over the ocean runs more smoothly and less wastefully because modern ports have larger places for ships to stop.

USAGE CLUES:

- The "link/connection" meaning is close to the "basic" meaning of *characteristic* ("typical, usual, or as something normally is"). Things that are typical of a thing or situation are linked to it without necessarily causing or resulting from it.
- It is best to learn the full phrase—with *of*—to focus on the "link/correlation" meaning. When the adjective appears without *of*, its meaning shifts away from "connected" and toward the basic meaning of "typical or usual."
- Always followed by a noun phrase naming a larger thing (e.g., see In Context 1 "low-wage economies, and In Context 2, modern port facilities") with which a smaller thing is connected. This is logically necessary, since a characteristic is a feature of a larger thing—only a part of its larger nature.
- Often in a reduced relative clause (see In Context 2, which is a reduced form of "the larger docks [which are] characteristic of modern port facilities")

To Help You Remember:

Comes from a Greek root meaning "make a mark on something by stamping or by carving with a sharp instrument." The connection to the modern meaning is that a characteristic is like a special sign that marks something. Think of characters in a movie or TV show. Each has things he or she usually does—things that are characteristic of that character.

associated with

Form	Common Related Forms
Verbal adjective + preposition	*association* (noun, usually uncountable in this meaning) *associate* (verb, usually transitive in this meaning)

In Context 1

Surprisingly, the questionnaire revealed that, within this <u>population</u>, success as a restaurant manager was strongly associated with a love of <u>cello</u> music.

In Other Words

After analyzing people's answers to a set of questions, we were surprised to see that, among people in this group, someone who does well at managing a restaurant is likely to enjoy music played on a cello (a stringed instrument like a violin but much larger and with a lower sound).

In Context 2

The PCC's report <u>emphasized</u> the low <u>birthrates</u> associated with <u>affluent</u>, service-based economies.

In Other Words

The PCC's report made a strong point that, in rich countries that make most of their money by providing services (instead of by producing goods or growing crops), it is very likely that, for each adult in the society, only a small number of children are being born each year.

USAGE CLUES:

- In this meaning, it is better to learn the verbal adjective (*associated*) than the base verb (*associate*). The verbal adjective is a reduced passive form that is much more common, in this meaning, than the active verb.
- Usually occurs either after a "linking" verb (*be, become, appear,* etc.), as in In Context 1 or in a reduced relative clause (see In Context 2).
- An adverb—*strongly, weakly, closely, intimately,* or *often*—is common before *associated* (see In Context 1).

Group 4. Connective phrases that relate two things often found together

in conjunction with

Form	Common Related Forms
Complex preposition	None

In Context 1

Archaeologists have found that remains of a grain called <u>millet</u> appear in conjunction with other traces of Malayo-Polynesian peoples.

In Other Words

If you find other signs of Malayo-Polynesian settlements, you will probably also find some old pieces of millet.

In Context 2

<u>Freckles</u>, in conjunction with reddish hair and light-colored eyes, hint at Nordic ancestry.

In Other Words

If someone has freckles (small dark spots on the skin) as well as reddish hair and light-colored eyes, some of that person's ancestors may have been from the area near present-day Sweden, Denmark, and Norway.

USAGE CLUES:

- Usually introduces an adverbial phrase, to modify a verb
- In some cases, a phrase starting with *in conjunction with* can act as an adjective (see In Context 2).
- Is used most often with visible conditions or events, things that can be observed

To Help You Remember:

Conjunction comes from Latin roots meaning "join together." If something occurs in conjunction with something else, they join together in that situation.

to the degree that

Form	Common Related Forms
Subordinator	None

In Context 1

Surprisingly enough, to the degree that a respondent was trained in a foreign language, he or she opposed <u>immigration</u>.

In Other Words

As foreign-language study increased, so did opposition to foreigners coming to one's own country and making it their new home.

In Context 2

The bacteria's motion increased to the degree that they consumed nutrients.

In Other Words

The more the bacteria ate, the more they moved around.

USAGE CLUES:

- Using a structure with *to the degree that* is like saying "as much as they do one thing, that is how much they will do another."
- Always followed by a clause
- *To the degree that* + clause can come either before the clause it modifies (see In Context 1) or after it (see In Context 2).

Consolidation Exercises: Groups 3 and 4

6.3. Collocations. Fill each blank with a word or phrase that goes well with the key vocabulary item. There are several possible answers to items 3, 4, and 5. *Hint:* Look at the Usage Clues and consider some of the additional vocabulary introduced in this section.

1. Psychological studies have shown that heavy smoking in the teen years

   _____ associated with certain

   undesirable personality traits, such as lack of self-confidence.

2. If you become good friends with someone who has Tourette's syndrome, you

   eventually get used to the noises and sudden movements _____

   _____ characteristic of the condition.

3. To the degree that a society values its natural environment, _____

   _____.

4. To provide effective security at large events like football games, you have to

   _____ in conjunction with

   careful observation of anyone who seems eager to start a fight.

5. _____ is associated with rapid

   development of suburbs on the edges of large cities.

6.4. Rephrasing. Using *characteristic of, associated with, in conjunction with,* or *to the degree that,* rephrase each of the following passages (write it in other words). You may change the form of the item you use to fit the grammar of what you write. Change the words of the original passage as much as necessary but don't change the meaning.

1. Wherever you find natural hot springs or geysers, you are also likely to experience frequent small earthquakes.

2. The more control workers have in the planning of their own time, the more loyal they are to the company for which they work.

3. Animals that produce huge numbers of young and do so very frequently tend to be very small and to have very short life spans.

4. A huge majority of the people who listen to public radio and watch public television in the United States have at least a bachelor's degree.

5. In the Great Lakes region, any place where people can easily find old arrow-heads and pieces of Indian pottery is likely to be near Indian burial mounds.

Group 5. Verbs that mean "indicate a connection" or "see indications of a connection"

imply

Form	Common Related Forms
Verb (transitive)	*implication* (noun, countable) *implicit* (adjective)

In Context 1

In yellow-rumped warblers (a kind of bird), a white throat implies one kind of song and a yellow throat implies another.

In Other Words

All those warblers with white throats sing one way, and all those with yellow throats sing another way.

In Context 2

North European ancestry implies that someone will have the genetic ability to produce <u>lactase</u>—an enzyme that helps digest milk—even in <u>adulthood</u>.

In Other Words

If someone has ancestors from northern Europe, that person's body is very likely to be able to produce lactase even after that person is fully grown.

USAGE CLUES:

- Some common subjects: conditions, events, situations, visible characteristics
- In this meaning, the subject of *imply* cannot be a human. If *imply* has a human subject, most readers will understand the verb as meaning "to mean something without saying it directly."
- The same is true if the subject is a noun for words or statements (*report, comment,* etc.); in statements about correlations or links, avoid using this kind of noun as the subject.
- The object of *imply* is often a clause beginning with *that* (see In Context 2).

- The noun *implication* is often followed by an *of* phrase (e.g., "One strong *implication* of north European ancestry is the ability to digest milk easily, even as an adult").
- The adjective *implicit* is often followed by an *in* phrase (e.g., "The ability to digest milk easily, even as an adult, is strongly *implicit* in north European ancestry").

 To Help You Remember:

Comes from Latin roots meaning "to fold in." An everyday connection: You may see <u>two-ply</u> paper towels or toilet paper—with two sheets "folded" together as one—in the grocery store. Remember that <u>pliers</u> can be used to bend ("fold") things.

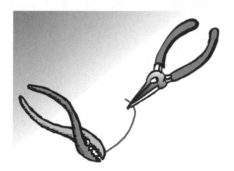 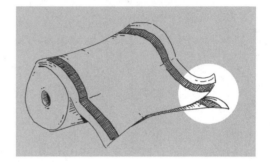

infer

Form	Common Related Forms
Verb (transitive)	*inference* (noun, countable/uncountable)

In Context 1

From the rapid growth of <u>algae</u> in this pond, we can infer a sudden inflow of organic material.

In Other Words

By seeing that algae (small, rootless plants that grow in large groups in water) have grown very quickly, we can conclude that organic matter (containing carbon and probably coming from a living thing) has flowed into the pond (a small lake) from somewhere.

In Context 2

By observing the pattern of disease <u>outbreaks</u>, officials inferred that mosquitoes probably carried the infectious agent.

In Other Words

By seeing where and when the disease showed up in large numbers of people, officials were able to conclude that mosquitoes (a kind of insect) carried the microorganism that made people sick.

USAGE CLUES:

- The subject is always human, because *infer* involves the ability to draw conclusions from evidence.
- In contexts of links or connections, often appears with a modal like *can* or *should* (see In Context 1)
- A *from* phrase (see In Context 1) or a phrase with *by* + verb-ing (see In Context 2) often names the evidence that allows a person to come to a conclusion.
- The object is often a *that* clause (see In Context 2).
- *BE CAREFUL:* Many people confuse *infer* with *imply.* Remember that the evidence IMPLIES something. You INFER something by looking at evidence.

Consolidation Exercises: Group 5

6.5. Meanings and Connections. Next to each meaning or description, write *imply* or *infer*—whichever best matches.

_____ 1. comes from a Latin root meaning "fold in"

_____ 2. The subject has to be a person or group of people.

_____ 3. In this meaning, the subject should not be a person or a statement.

6.6. Collocations. Fill each blank with a word or phrase that goes well with the key vocabulary item. There are several possible answers to items 3 and 4. *Hint:* Look at the Usage Clues and consider some of the additional vocabulary introduced in this section.

1. The broken window and disorder in the room implied _____

_____ a burglary had occurred.

2. We were able to infer, _____ the

rapid solidification of the mixture, that a "seed crystal" had somehow entered

the container.

3. The presence of a large number of protesters at the meeting of the World Financial

Council implied _____.

4. By looking at the marks on the dead person's body and by doing a medical examination, doctors inferred _____

_____ .

6.7. Rephrasing. Using *imply* or *infer,* rephrase each of the following passages (write it in other words). You may change the form of the item you use to fit the grammar of what you write. Change the words of the original passage as much as necessary but don't change the meaning.

1. The article had been published in the most important British journal of science, and most readers believed that the information in it was reliable.

2. Most of the people suffering from Montego fever were found to have high levels of a chemical called sybillomasine in their blood.

3. When you are looking at a satellite photograph of the Earth and you see that an area of high clouds looks very wavy, it is very likely that strong upper-level winds are blowing over that area.

4. When I walked into the meeting, I could tell from the looks on people's faces that I was in serious trouble.

👁 Comprehensive Review Exercises

6.8. Matching. Next to each item in the left column, write the letter of the best meaning or description from the right column. Do not use any letter more than once.

____	1.	link
____	2.	correlation
____	3.	accompany
____	4.	go along with
____	5.	characteristic of
____	6.	associated with
____	7.	in conjunction with
____	8.	to the degree that
____	9.	imply
____	10.	infer

a. in this meaning, should not have a human subject; comes from Latin root meaning "fold in"

b. in this meaning, should not have a human subject; comes from Latin roots meaning "to go along with, especially as a friend"

c. is always followed by a clause

d. is often followed by *between . . . and, to,* or *with*

e. must have a human subject, because it involves drawing conclusions

f. is a complex preposition, always followed by a noun phrase

g. comes from a Greek root meaning "make a mark on something by stamping or by carving with a sharp instrument"

h. In a technical usage of this word, a number with a decimal point in it might indicate how frequently things go together.

i. is a combination of three very common English words—a two-word verb + a preposition

j. is a verb that, in this meaning, usually occurs as a reduced passive, not in the active form

6.9. Connections. Name some things that are connected to or that are often found with each of the following. Try to name things that are not necessarily a cause or an effect of the event or situation.

1. a major holiday (e.g., Halloween, Thanksgiving, Chinese New Year)

2. a very long airplane trip from east to west (e.g., from the U.S. to Asia)

3. a very strong economy

4. feeling good about your job

5. growing old

6.10. Usage Practice. Based on what you already know about the key vocabulary, fill each blank in Column A with one of the words from Column B. Do not use any item from Column B more than once.

Column A	Column B
1. There is a strong _____ between smoking and certain diseases.	imply
	associated
2. Researchers found that, among voters in Garden City, a distrust of government was _____ with high levels of education.	accompanied
	link
	infer
3. By looking at these data, I can _____ that the region is not good for growing grapes.	
4. These data _____ that the region is not good for growing grapes.	
5. In people suffering from Franke's syndrome, a feeling of personal inadequacy is often _____ by other fears and anxieties.	

6.11. Fitting In. Choose the best word or phrase to complete each sentence. Write it in the blank.

Example: Because of the heavy rain, we had to <u>alter</u> our plans. (mutate, transform, alter)

1. The police chief pointed out the high _____ between gang violence and tougher laws against drugs. (link, correlation, degree)

2. Most people who die in burning buildings are killed not by the fire itself but by the smoke _____ with it. (associated, characteristic, in conjunction)

3. Having a car insurance policy _____ that a person has not only a car but also, probably, a driver's license. (implies, infers, goes along with)

4. In most countries, a falling birthrate is _____ a rise in per capita income. (associated with, to the degree that, characteristic of)

5. A new study found that, _____ a person enjoyed elementary school, he or she is likely to choose teaching as a career. Those who had good early experiences in school are very likely to desire a teaching career, whereas those who disliked school have little chance of choosing to become teachers. (to the degree that, in conjunction with, characteristic of)

6. Although some people think video games encourage violence, researchers have found no _____ violent behavior and the amount of time spent playing video games. (link between, correlation with, link to)

6.12. Combinations and Collocations. Fill in each blank with a word or phrase that fits well with the key vocabulary item. Many answers are possible for items 4–10.

1. More work needs to be done to explain alcoholism's apparent link _____ _____ one's genetic makeup.

2. Somewhat paradoxically, forest fires in the western U.S. _____ _____ in conjunction with periods of frequent thunderstorms.

3. Although no one has ever proven that a high-fiber diet can prevent colon cancer, there is a(n) _____ correlation between fiber intake and the disease.

4. _____ inferred from the suspect's appearance, speech, and overall behavior that he had been taking illegal drugs.

5. A lowering of the voice and an increase in oiliness of a boy's skin and hair are characteristic of _____.

6. The drug company's representatives denied that there was any correlation between _____ and

_____.

7. Child psychologists advised parents not to give their children creative and unusual names, because they claimed that _____

_____ was strongly associated with having a name that makes a child stand out among other children.

8. To the degree that _____, a society risks a violent upheaval like revolution or a military coup.

9. _____ implies a blockage somewhere in the pipes that carry water away from the house to the sewage system.

10. In our solar system, there is a link between a planet's size and _____

_____.

6.13. Building with Key Vocabulary. Each item names two things. Use the key vocabulary item in brackets and write a short passage (one or two sentences) to state that there is—or isn't, or sometimes is—a link or correlation between the two things. Change the wording as necessary to suit your passage.

1. height/skill in playing basketball [link]

2. a desire to dress differently from one's parents/becoming a teenager [go along with]

3. low levels of blood sugar/a feeling of tiredness [accompany]

4. red hair/freckles [associated with]

5. an increase in security checks at the airport/a visit by the pope [in conjunction with]

6. extremely high levels of cholesterol in the blood/a poor diet [imply]

7. unhappiness in one's job/trouble in one's marriage [correlation]

8. a highly mobile population/societies that place a high value on success in one's job [characteristic of] *Note: highly mobile* = moving frequently (probably from one city to another).

9. corruption in government/foreign companies are reluctant to invest [to the degree that]

10. growing demand for traditional Asian medicines/threat to the populations of certain animals (such as sun bears and rhinoceroses) [infer]

Additional Vocabulary for Chapter 6

The additional words and phrases that have come up in the In Context examples in chapter 6 can be found in Appendix 1. (They are underlined when they occur in the In Context sections.) These terms are not fully explained, but you should be able to understand them from the contexts and brief explanations that are given. Do the exercises below to help solidify your understanding of these words and phrases.

6.14. Additional Vocabulary 1: Meanings. In each blank, write the letter of the meaning from Column B that goes best with each vocabulary item in Column A.

Column A

_____ 1. millet
_____ 2. cello
_____ 3. ache
_____ 4. outbreak
_____ 5. adulthood
_____ 6. time zone
_____ 7. emphasize
_____ 8. wage
_____ 9. fever
_____ 10. affluent
_____ 11. chain
_____ 12. birthrate
_____ 13. pliers
_____ 14. lactase
_____ 15. immigration

Column B

a. being fully grown
b. The time is later or earlier in the next one.
c. a high body temperature
d. made of links
e. This helps people digest milk.
f. used for bending something
g. moving to a new country, to stay there
h. pain
i. used for playing music
j. You can eat this grain.
k. the number of children being born, as compared to the number of adults
l. say very strongly or forcefully
m. rich
n. an _____ of a disease
o. pay

6.15. Additional Vocabulary 2: Fitting into Sentences. Fill each blank on page 142 with one of the additional vocabulary items from the list below. You may have to change the form of an item to fit the grammar of the sentence. Do not use any item more than once. Some items will not be used at all.

affluent	depression	population
algae	freckle	suicide
bald	jet lag	time zone
cello	outbreak	two-ply
coincidence	pliers	

1. Elizabeth gets _____ on her face if she stays out in the sun for a long time.

2. The water in the pond looked green because a lot of _____ had grown during the warm weather.

3. The sound of a(n) _____ is like that of a violin but deeper.

4. Sorry, but I'm feeling really tired. I just got off an 18-hour flight from India, and I've got _____ .

5. The _____ of the Lansing metropolitan area has grown by about 15% in the last ten years.

6. Greg always wears a hat when he goes outside in the middle of the day, because he's _____ and would get a bad sunburn on his head if he didn't.

7. In earlier years, people who complained of long-lasting sadness and a feeling that life had no purpose were routinely sent to psychiatrists. Now, such _____ is typically treated by drugs that can be prescribed by any medical doctor.

8. Single sheets of paper toweling are not strong enough for most cleaning jobs, so I usually buy _____ towels.

9. Most life insurance policies will not pay any money if a person's death is officially declared a(n) _____ .

10. By a very odd _____ , there were three people named Mary Johnson among the twenty people in the class.

▌▌ Writing Projects

6.16. Writing Projects. The following are some suggestions for writing projects that will allow you to use the key vocabulary and some of the additional vocabulary. Each of the topics could be lightly covered in an essay of 500–600 words more thoroughly in a paper of 1,500–2,000 words. To write information-packed longer papers you should do some research in the library and /or on the Internet.

1. Think of a time when—only by looking at certain clues or evidence—you knew that something had happened. (For example, it is sometimes possible to walk into a room and know, just by looking at people's faces, that something very bad has happened.) Use the key vocabulary to describe such a situation.

2. Some people speak of a "digital divide" that separates some societies from others. On one side of the divide are "online" societies in which many (perhaps most) people have access to the Internet and other electronic communication resources. On the other side are "offline" societies in which such access is rare, perhaps available only to a few rich or powerful persons. Write an essay in which you use the key vocabulary to describe the characteristics of societies on one or both sides of this divide. You can choose to describe only online societies, only offline societies, or both. Please concentrate on those characteristics or conditions that occur together but are not necessarily causes of or results of one another. Doing so will give you a better chance to exercise the vocabulary in this unit. In addition to these noncausal links, you will probably also mention some cause-effect relationships. For help with the vocabulary related to these, you may want to look at chapter 7, "Causes and Effects."

3. Using the questions on page 144, survey at least 10 people (more if possible) about their eating and drinking habits. Then write a report about some of the correlations you discover from your survey. For example, is there any relationship between someone's home country and what he or she eats for breakfast?

Background

1. Sex: Female ___   Male ___   2. Age____   3. Home country_____

4. Marital status: Single ___   Married ___   Separated ___   Divorced ___   Widowed ___

5. Parental status: Number of children _____

   Ages of children ____, ____, ____, ____, ____, ____,

6. Field of study (present or expected) _____

7. Religion _____ (optional)

Eating and Drinking Habits

Circle the number that best describes how often you do each of the following.

	Never	Almost Never	Sometimes	Often	Very Often
I. For breakfast I					
drink coffee	1	2	3	4	5
eat eggs	1	2	3	4	5
eat bacon or ham	1	2	3	4	5
eat cereal	1	2	3	4	5
eat bread or toast	1	2	3	4	5
eat rice	1	2	3	4	5
eat noodles	1	2	3	4	5
II. I eat a big lunch.	1	2	3	4	5
III. For dinner I					
drink coffee	1	2	3	4	5
eat meat	1	2	3	4	5
eat rice	1	2	3	4	5
eat noodles	1	2	3	4	5
IV. I drink					
beer	1	2	3	4	5
wine	1	2	3	4	5
whiskey	1	2	3	4	5
vodka	1	2	3	4	5
V. I eat at fast-food restaurants (e.g., Kentucky Fried Chicken, McDonald's, etc.)	1	2	3	4	5
VI. I cook my own dinner at home.	1	2	3	4	5

Chapter 7   **Causes and Effects**

This vocabulary may be useful when:

You want to go beyond connectives (e.g., *as a result, because of*) in writing about the causes of things. The following are all verbs (or verb phrases).

Key Vocabulary

Group 1	Group 2	Group 3	Group 4	Group 5
stem from	lead to	render	favor	be responsible for
be due to	yield	make	promote	provoke
derive from	generate			be blamed for

✥ Exploring the Vocabulary

Group 1. Verbs whose subject is the result

stem from

Form	Common Related Forms
Verb (intransitive) + preposition	None

In Context 1

The company's problems stemmed mostly from lax quality control.

In Other Words

The company had problems mostly because it didn't carefully make sure that its products were made properly.

In Context 2

Labor unrest, stemming from unsafe working conditions, was rampant early in the century.

In Other Words

In the early part of the century, there were many disturbances by workers unhappy about working in dangerous conditions.

USAGE CLUES:

- While the subject of the verb is a result, the object of the preposition (*from*) is the cause.
- Common subjects: feelings, situations, conditions, events
- Does not work well with a subject that is a physical object. For example, it would sound strange to say, "Coastal fog stems from a moist wind off the sea."
- An adverb of degree (*mostly, largely,* etc.) often comes between *stem* and *from.*

be due to

Form	Common Related Forms
Verb + adjective + preposition	None

In Context 1

Delays in the research schedule were due primarily to funding problems.

In Context 2

Coastal fog is due to a moist onshore airflow.

In Other Words

Problems with getting money were the main reason why the research didn't go as fast as expected.

In Other Words

Wet air blowing to land from the ocean causes fog along the coast.

USAGE CLUES:

- You should learn *be due to*—not simply *due to*—so you can avoid an old usage controversy: some readers object to *due to* phrases as sentence modifiers (e.g., "Our flight was canceled due to bad weather"). These critics would say, "owing to bad weather" or, even safer, "as a result of bad weather" instead. They insist that a phrase with *due to* acts as an adjective and must clearly modify a noun (e.g., our flight's cancellation due to bad weather"). If you use *due to* with a form of *be*—or where one is understood—you won't offend these readers.
- An adverb of degree (such as *primarily, largely, mostly*) often comes before or after *due* (see In Context 1).
- Some common subjects: feelings, conditions, events
- Unlike *stem from* can have a concrete thing as the subject, usually if the name of a process follows *due to* (see In Context 2)

derive from

Form	Common Related Forms
Verb (intransitive in this meaning) + preposition	*derivative of* (adjective + preposition) *derivation from* (noun + preposition)

In Context 1
Most stomach ulcers derive from infection by a <u>bacterium</u>, not from stress.

In Other Words
Most stomach ulcers come from (are caused by) infection by this bacterium, not from stress.

In Context 2
Richardson claims that Africa's current problems derive from nineteenth-century <u>colonialism</u>.

In Other Words
Richardson claims that foreign control of African territories in the 1800s is the basic cause of today's problems.

USAGE CLUES:

- While the subject of the verb (always intransitive in this meaning) is a result, the object of the preposition (*from*) is the cause.
- Works well in describing a somewhat slow or long process of causing
- Has a strong sense of "coming from X," "having X as its source or origin"
- Strangely, a related transitive form of *derive* can appear in the passive without much changing the meaning (e.g., "most stomach ulcers are derived from infection by"). The implication is "derived [by somebody]."

Group 2. Subject is the cause; no special emphasis

lead to

Form	Common Related Forms
Verb (intransitive) + preposition	None

In Context 1

He then discovered he had been <u>infected</u> with HIV, the virus that can lead to AIDS.

In Other Words

Then he found that the human immuno-deficiency virus (which can eventually cause AIDS) had entered his body and begun reproducing there.

In Context 2

An excess of nutrients in the water can lead to oxygen imbalance, which can eventually lead to the <u>collapse</u> of the entire aquatic system.

In Other Words

Too many nutrients in the water can cause the amount of oxygen in the water to be wrong. This can then cause the whole system of living things in the water to fall apart.

USAGE CLUES:

- Works well in context of a "causal chain"—a process with several steps, each of which causes another (e.g., "X leads to Y, which leads to Z") (see In Context 2)
- An adverb showing speed or frequency often comes before or after *lead* (e.g., "leads eventually to," "often leads to," etc.).
- Like other verbs in this group, goes well with *can* or *may* to express a cause-effect relationship that sometimes happens, sometimes doesn't
- There is a related causal form in which *lead* is transitive and *to* is NOT a preposition but part of an infinitive. This related usage involves the pattern *lead* + noun phrase + *to* + verb—e.g., *leads me to believe,* which means "causes me to believe."

yield

Form	Common Related Forms
Verb (transitive)	*yield* (noun, countable)

In Context 1

A medical student's <u>sacrifices</u> early in life yield substantial rewards later.

In Context 2

<u>Automating</u> the car industry yielded great improvements in quality control.

In Other Words

For someone studying to be a medical doctor, doing without some comforts early in life [so he or she can concentrate on studying] will give that person big rewards later.

In Other Words

Because most processes in making cars were controlled by machines, it seemed easier to make sure the cars were of high quality.

USAGE CLUES:

- Has a strong sense of "produce" or create through a process
- Is common in the reading of chemical formulas. For example, the formula $CO_2 + 2H_2O \rightarrow O_2 + CH_2O + H_2O$ would be read as "C O two plus two H two O yields O two plus C H two O plus H two O."
- Common objects: *result, increase, rewards, improvement, benefit, little,* terms for money
- Common subjects: words for actions, conditions, events

generate

Form	Common Related Forms
Verb (transitive)	*generation* (noun, uncountable in this meaning) *generative* (adjective)

In Context 1

Rodrigues's presidential <u>campaign</u> generated great excitement in the villages.

In Context 2

Sales of <u>licensed products</u> generated more income than the movie itself.

In Other Words

Rodrigues's attempt to become president caused a lot of excitement among people in villages.

In Other Words

More money was made by selling things related to the movie (e.g., toys, T-shirts, etc.) than by selling tickets to the movie.

USAGE CLUES:

- Common subjects: actions, processes, events
- Common objects: terms for speech, emotions, forces, or money
- Can carry a sense of
    "giving birth"
    "making something that seems electric or powerful"

- Often appears in contexts about what computers produce. A *computer-generated image* is a picture created by using a computer.
- Also often appears in contexts about electrical power. A machine that makes electricity is called a generator.

 To Help You Remember:

Comes from a Latin root meaning "to produce, especially to produce children." Notice the similarity to words about having children—*gene, generation,* etc.

As They Say

Where there's smoke, there's fire.

Even if you can't easily see the cause of something, the cause must exist.

For example:

A: "Our sales are down but our marketing strategy seems strong."
B: "Where there's smoke, there's fire."

Speaker B is implying that maybe there is something wrong with the marketing strategy. After all, *something* must be causing the sales problem.

Consolidation Exercises: Groups 1 and 2

7.1. Usage Practice. Fill each blank with one of the key vocabulary items. You may have to change the form of the item to fit the grammar of the sentence. There are several possible answers to some. *Hint:* Look at the Usage Clues and consider some of the additional vocabulary introduced in this section.

1. Our fascination with high-tech warfare _____ an inability to face the moral implications of war.

2. Jack's long hours in the office _____ little profit for either him or the company.

3. The product's failure _____ mostly _____

_____ inadequate marketing.

4. The orange glow that you see in this kind of streetlight _____
_____ the sodium vapor in the lamp.

5. A new interest in Egyptian history was _____ by the
museum's exhibit of ancient artifacts.

6. Loss of coolant _____ a huge buildup of heat and an
eventual warping of the reactor's control rods.

7.2. Rephrasing. Using *stem from, be due to, derive from, lead to, yield,* or
generate, rephrase each of the following passages (write it in other words).
You may change the form of the item you use to fit the grammar of what you
write. Change the words of the original passage as much as necessary but
don't change the meaning.

1. Public demand for compact discs caused hard times for the makers of vinyl
record albums.

2. Careful attention to detail in the experiment resulted in highly reliable findings.

3. If someone feels ill after drinking milk, the problem is probably that the person
has a hard time digesting milk, not that the person has an allergy.

4. Latin was very important in all fields of study during the Renaissance, as a result
of the language's association with the still-powerful Catholic Church.

5. Increasing the amount of sugar in the mixture causes the yeast to produce more
carbon dioxide.

6. By hiring more and more part-time workers, the university caused great anxiety
to develop among its full-time staff.

Group 3. Can mean "cause someone/something to become"

render

Form	Common Related Forms
Verb (complex transitive)	None in this meaning

In Context 1

Corruption in the police force rendered the drug laws ineffective.

In Other Words

Dishonest activity among the police caused the laws against drugs to become ineffective.

In Context 2

A tough question from a reporter rendered the president speechless.

In Other Words

A difficult question from a reporter caused the president to become speechless (disturbed her so much that she couldn't think of anything to say).

USAGE CLUES:

- The direct object of *render* must be followed by an object complement—something that completes the thought about the direct object. This object complement is usually an adjective (see In Context 1 and 2).
- The adjective that follows the direct object usually indicates an undesirable quality. It most often means "weak" or "deficient."
- Because the sense is usually negative, the direct object of *render* is usually a "victim" of the subject. The subject is doing something bad or harmful to the object.
- In rare cases, the object complement can be a noun phrase instead of an adjective (e.g., "rendered the rules a joke"), but this is relatively uncommon.

make

Form	Common Related Forms
Verb (complex transitive)	None

In Context 1

Currency <u>devaluation</u> makes imports more expensive.

In Other Words

Drops in the value of a country's currency cause imports to be more expensive.

In Context 2

Retirements and resignations made Sue Williams the most <u>senior</u> employee in the office.

In Other Words

Because many people either retired or resigned, Williams became the longest-serving employee in the office.

USAGE CLUES:

- The direct object of *make* must be followed by an object complement— something that completes the thought about the direct object. This object complement can be a noun phrase (see In Context 2), an adjective (see In Context 1), or the base form of a verb (e.g., "The memory of his mother made him cry").
- If the object complement is an adjective, it could indicate either good or bad qualities. (This is one usage difference between *render* and *make*.)
- If the object complement is a noun phrase, it will always carry a sense of status, position, or identity. (See In Context 2, where the object complement [*the most senior employee in the office*] indicates a status.)
- Can also take a simple noun phrase as its object, especially in certain fixed expressions (e.g., "make trouble," "make a mess").
- Be careful to avoid possible confusion with other meanings of *make*, especially the meaning "make X for Y." For example, *It made him a better friend* could have two meanings—"caused him to be a better friend" and "created a better friend for him." Context would probably make it clear which meaning you wanted, but a reader could find the double meaning funny.

Group 4. Verbs that emphasize that the subject (the cause) doesn't always lead to the result

favor

Form	Common Related Forms
Verb (transitive)	*favorable* (adjective) **NOT** in this meaning: *favorite* (adjective/noun), *favor* (noun)

In Context 1

Heat and an oxygen-poor environment favor the formation of long, <u>opaque</u> crystals.

In Other Words

Conditions in which there is a lot of heat and there isn't much oxygen are likely to cause the formation of long crystals that light won't pass through.

In Context 2

Strict antidrug laws tend to favor an underground economy controlled by <u>gangs</u>.

In Other Words

Strict laws against drugs are likely to result in a system of trade that is hidden from most people and is controlled by organized groups of criminals.

USAGE CLUES:

- To *favor* X is to "create conditions that support X."
- Carries a sense of likeliness or high probability. Works well in contexts of a statistical chance.
- Fits well in writing that has a technical tone (see In Context 1)
- Common objects: terms for processes (*formation, development, growth*, etc), terms for the results of a process
- Common subjects: terms for conditions, rules, events
- Do not use a term for a living thing or a group of living things as the subject of *favor* in this meaning. (With a subject like that, *favor* has a different meaning ["like" or "prefer"].)
- Often used after *tend to* (see In Context 2)

promote

Form	Common Related Forms
Verb (transitive)	*promotion* (noun, uncountable in this meaning)

In Context 1

<u>Flexible</u> scheduling promotes a sense of personal responsibility among staff members.

In Other Words

Allowing staff members to set their own schedules tends to make them feel personally responsible for the success of their work.

In Context 2

Ultraviolet radiation promotes the growth of melanoma.

In Other Words

Ultraviolet radiation commonly leads to the growth of dark tumors on the skin.

USAGE CLUES:

- Common subjects: terms for conditions or processes
- Common objects: terms for processes (*growth, development*, etc.). The object could also be a product that might result from a process (e.g., "promotes melanoma").
- In this meaning, neither the subject nor the object should be a living thing. Persons as subjects or objects will imply other meanings of "promote."

 To Help You Remember:

Comes from a Latin root meaning "move forward."

Consolidation Exercises: Groups 3 and 4

7.3. Collocations. Fill each blank with a word or phrase that goes well with the key vocabulary item. There are several possible answers to each. *Hint:* Look at the Usage Clues and consider some of the additional vocabulary introduced in this section.

    1. Fumes from overheated electric wires made 17 workers _____

        _____ .

    2. Shorter days and cooler nights favor _____ in leaf

        color from green to yellow.

    3. Open communication between husband and wife promotes _____

        _____ .

    4. His lack of computer skills rendered him _____ .

7.4. Rephrasing. Using *render, make, favor,* or *promote,* rephrase each of the following passages (write it in other words). You may change the form of the item you use to fit the grammar of what you write. Change the words of the original passage as much as necessary but don't change the meaning.

    1. Researchers found that a lack of decision-making power caused workers to perform less efficiently.

2. Strong upper-level winds and high humidity provide good conditions for tornadoes to form.

3. Small, windowless rooms cause some people to become anxious and fearful.

4. Easy access to iron and coal helped a steel industry develop near the Great Lakes.

5. Conditions in the eastern Caribbean Sea now are likely to cause hurricanes to form.

Group 5. Verbs that imply the object (a result) is unpleasant or undesirable

be responsible for

Form	Common Related Forms
Verb + adjective + preposition	None

In Context 1

Nickel mining is responsible for the deadliest pollutants in Aconnak River.

In Other Words

The most harmful pollutants in the river come from nickel (Ni) mines.

In Context 2

Unexpectedly high temperatures were responsible for <u>deterioration</u> of the rubber seals.

In Other Words

The weakening or breakdown of the rubber seals occurred because they got hotter than expected. (Seals help fill the space between two parts of a machine or a building.)

USAGE CLUES:

- Common subjects: terms for conditions, events, activities—a wide range of possibilities
- A human subject gives the phrase an added implication of "moral accountability."

- The object is often a term for something undesirable (see In Context 1 and 2).
- Even if the object is a term for something not usually undesirable, *be responsible for* may imply something wrong about it (e.g., "Everyone knew what was responsible for his promotion"—the reader assumes that the promotion was bad in some way, perhaps unearned).

provoke

Form	Common Related Forms
Verb (transitive)	*provocative* (adjective) *provocation* (noun)

In Context 1

The new tax laws provoked an angry response.

In Other Words

The new tax laws caused people to react angrily.

In Context 2

By refusing to meet with the worker's representatives, management provoked a two-week <u>strike</u>.

In Other Words

Because the managers refused to meet with their representatives, the workers refused to work, and this continued for two weeks.

USAGE CLUES:

- Common objects—unpleasant feelings, unpleasant events (e.g., *retaliation*)
- The meaning changes if the "object" is a human (or some other animal). Then it means "make angry."
- Works only when the object is a term for some kind of reaction or response—usually a negative one
- Common subjects: terms for events, rules, speech, actions, etc. Human subjects are possible (see In Context 2).

be blamed for

Form	Common Related Forms
Verb (passive) + preposition	*blame* (noun, uncountable) *be blamed on* (see Usage Clues)

In Context 1

Slash-and-burn farming has been blamed for many of Asia's brushfires.

In Other Words

Someone claims that many of the fires in brush-covered areas of Asia are caused by farming methods that clear land by burning the plants.

In Context 2

Stress had long been blamed for most stomach ulcers.

In Other Words

For a long time, people used to say that stress caused most stomach ulcers.

USAGE CLUES:

- Has a meaning of "people say" along with a meaning of "causing"
- You can focus more strongly on the "causing" meaning by using this passive without a *by* phrase (see In Context 1 and 2).
- It's possible to emphasize the "people say" meaning by changing to the active voice (e.g., "Doctors blamed stress for most stomach ulcers") or by adding a *by* phrase (e.g., "Stress was blamed by doctors for most stomach ulcers").
- Common subjects: conditions, people, events
- The related form *be blamed on* takes the result as its subject and the cause as the object of the *on* phrase.

Consolidation Exercises: Group 5

7.5. Collocations. Fill each blank with a word or phrase that goes well with the key vocabulary item. There are several possible answers for item 3. *Hint:* Look at the Usage Clues and consider some of the additional vocabulary introduced in this section.

1. The floods were responsible _____ 16 deaths.

2. Sixteen deaths were blamed _____ the floods.

3. Distrust between the two groups provoked _____.

4. Poor accounting controls are largely responsible _____

_____ the bank's failure.

5. High temperatures were blamed _____ the

deterioration of the rubber seals.

7.6. Rephrasing. Using *be responsible for, provoke,* or *be blamed for,* rephrase each of the following passages (write it in other words). You may change the form of the item you use to fit the grammar of what you write. Change the words of the original passage as much as necessary but don't change the meaning.

1. High winds caused the grass fires to spread quickly.

2. At one time, people used to say that mental illness was caused by evil spirits.

3. The front panel warped (bent or twisted) because a great deal of pressure built up behind it.

4. The investigators identified pilot error as the cause of the crash.

5. The students loudly denied breaking the window after the teacher accused them of doing so.

6. The children failed to return before dark. This caused the parents to become very worried.

👁 Comprehensive Review Exercises

7.7. Matching. Next to each item in the left column, write the letter of the best description from the right column. Do not use any letter more than once.

_____ 1. stem from

_____ 2. be due to

_____ 3. lead to

_____ 4. yield

_____ 5. generate

_____ 6. render

_____ 7. derive from

_____ 8. make

_____ 9. favor

_____ 10. promote

_____ 11. be responsible for

_____ 12. provoke

_____ 13. be blamed for

a. combines the meanings "people say" and "causing"

b. often used in describing causal chains; has a basic meaning of "showing the way"

c. Even if the object is something usually good, this vocabulary item may imply something bad about it.

d. Its object will be a noun followed by another noun, a verb, or an adjective.

e. Its object is a term for a reaction or response.

f. Its object is almost always a noun followed by an adjective implying weakness or deficiency.

g. is related to the name for a machine that makes electricity

h. has a basic meaning of "giving"; the cause "gives" the result

i. comes from the name for part of a plant

j. comes from a Latin root meaning "move forward"

k. has a sense of "create conditions that support"

l. Many readers don't like it if a writer drops "be" from this item.

m. has a sense of "comes off from a source, like a branch of a larger river"

7.8. Fitting In. Choose the best word or phrase to complete each sentence. Write it in the blank.

Example: Because of the heavy rain, we had to <u>alter</u> our plans. (mutate, transform, alter)

1. Production delays _____ frustration among the

   sales reps (rendered, made, provoked)

2. Last year's decision to build 150 new low-rent commercial buildings _____

   _____ great excitement among the area's small-business

   owners. (generated, provoked, was due to)

3. Extremely low temperatures can _____ copper a superconductive pathway. (be responsible for, lead to, make)

4. Poor construction of office buildings and high-rise apartments _____ _____ the huge death toll in last month's earthquake. (stemmed from, promoted, was responsible for)

5. Programs to _____ good communication between parents and teenagers can _____ great benefits for families and society. (make, promote, provoke) (be blamed for, yield, favor)

6. There is no evidence that using "soft" drugs like alcohol or marijuana _____ _____ the use of hard drugs like heroin. (leads to, favors, is responsible for)

7.9. Combinations and Collocations. Fill in each blank with a word or phrase that fits well with the key vocabulary item. Many answers are possible for each item.

1. Loud noises make me _____.

2. _____ stems from America's tradition of free speech.

3. Warm, moist weather promotes _____ _____.

4. The civil war in Grimaldia provoked _____ _____.

5. Poor maintenance of the ship and an inexperienced crew are being blamed for _____.

6. Mr. Fox's booming voice and grand gestures generated _____ _____.

7. Opposition from women's groups rendered the proposed law _____ _____.

8. Combining sulfuric acid (H_2SO_4) with water (H_2O) yields _____

   _____ .

9. _____ was due to the eruption

   of Mount Hermera, a volcano in western Indonesia.

10. Heavy rain was responsible for _____ .

Additional Vocabulary for Chapter 7

The additional words and phrases that have come up in the In Context examples in chapter 7 can be found in Appendix 1. (They are underlined when they occur in the In Context sections.) These terms are not fully explained, but you should be able to understand them from the contexts and brief explanations that are given. Do the exercises below to help solidify your understanding of these words and phrases.

7.10. Additional Vocabulary 1: Meanings. In each blank, write the letter of the meaning from column B that goes best with each vocabulary item in column A.

Column A

_____ 1. infect
_____ 2. gang
_____ 3. corruption
_____ 4. funding
_____ 5. quality control
_____ 6. strike
_____ 7. senior
_____ 8. licensed product
_____ 9. sacrifice
_____ 10. delay
_____ 11. lax
_____ 12. opaque

Column B

a. not strict
b. an action in which a large group of workers refuses to work
c. doing without nice things now so you can achieve some other important goal
d. having held a job for a long time
e. a product that shows a symbol or character from a movie, a sports team, etc.
f. money that supports an activity
g. lateness
h. dishonest activity
i. not letting light through
j. get into a person's body (what a disease-causing organism does)
k. a group, usually one involved in crime
l. making sure a product is made properly

7.11. Additional Vocabulary 2: Fitting into Sentences. Fill each blank with one of the additional vocabulary items from the list below. You may have to change the form of an item to fit the grammar of the sentence. Do not use any item more than once. Some items will not be used at all.

airflow	collapse	labor unrest
automate	colonialism	rampant
bacterium	devaluation	slash-and-burn
campaign	flexible	speechless

1. An antibiotic will help control a disease caused by a(n) _____

   _____ but not one caused by a virus.

2. President Mohandzir complained that foreign companies in his country were guilty of a new form of economic _____, because they exploited locals to make foreigners rich.

3. Cossetia was having trouble exporting its goods because the prices were too high. To make their prices more competitive, the Central Bank of Cossetia decided to _____ the local currency.

4. Many apartment buildings and office towers simply _____ _____ a few seconds after the earthquake started.

5. Even if an employer doesn't want any workers to lose their jobs, it's hard to resist the pressure to _____ production processes. Machines work a lot cheaper than people do.

6. Our research schedule is _____, so we can do our interviews whenever it would be convenient for you.

7. In America, the presidential _____ is virtually endless. As soon as a new president is elected, the opponents begin their efforts to succeed him or her.

8. The civil war crippled the nation. Clean water was rare, and waterborne diseases were _____ throughout the country.

9. If you open windows on two sides of the room, you can get better _____ _____ than if you open just one.

10. _____ in the northern coal-mining region severely reduced production and left the nation without enough fuel to last the winter.

¶ Writing Projects

7.12. Writing Projects. The following are some suggestions for writing projects that will allow you to use the key vocabulary and some of the additional vocabulary. Each of the topics could be lightly covered in an essay of 500–600 words or more thoroughly in a paper of 1,500–2,000 words. To write information-packed longer papers (especially about topics 4, 5, and 6) you should do some research in the library and/or on the Internet.

1. Think of an illness. Use the key vocabulary to describe what causes it.
2. Drop something (a pen, a ball, etc). Use the key vocabulary to describe what happened.
3. In your opinion, why do some children grow up to be especially successful? Use the key vocabulary to explain what leads to this success.
4. Some of the most unusual weather on record occurred in the last 10 years of the twentieth century. Many of the strongest storms, worst floods, and longest droughts (periods of little or no rain) occurred then. What do you think might be the reason(s) for this odd concentration of bad weather?
5. Financial markets have always fluctuated (gone up and down) in a cyclical way. There's a time when stock prices are up, then a time when they're down, then a time when they're up again.
    (a) Try to explain why this happens. (Even if you have not studied business or finance, you can use reason to figure this out.)
    (b) These cycles have been getting shorter. The ups and downs have been getting larger and have come more quickly since the early 1990s. Why might this be happening?
6. There are many different kinds of education systems worldwide. Some emphasize discipline; others emphasize freedom. Some emphasize memorization of facts; others emphasize creative discovery. But all aim for the same thing—to train young people for membership in the society. What in your opinion, is the best way to achieve this aim?

Chapter 8 **Permitting, Making Easier**

This vocabulary may be useful when:
You want to write about specific situations in which a process is made possible or made easier or faster. There are many vocabulary items beyond the common verb *let* that will help you express this.

Key Vocabulary

Group 1	Group 2	Group 3
permit	permissive	consent
allow	lenient	approval

Group 4	Group 5	Group 6
exempt	facilitate	clear the way for
excuse	ease	remove obstacles to

 Exploring the Vocabulary

Group 1. Verbs for "letting" in a broad, general sense

permit

Form	Common Related Forms
Verb (transitive)	*permission* (noun, usually countable) *permissible* (adjective meaning "able to be done because someone is likely to say it's okay") *permitted* (verbal adjective meaning "able to be done because someone has already said it's okay")

In Context 1

WTO regulations permit looser trade practices in developing countries.

In Other Words

The rules of the WTO let developing countries trade in ways that other countries may not.

In Context 2

Sending <u>personal</u> email messages from the office is not permitted; official business only.

In Other Words

You may send email messages from the office only if the message relates to work. You may not send private messages to your friends.

USAGE CLUES:

- Common subjects: terms for people, organizations, rules
- If the subject is a kind of condition, *permit* has a sense of "make possible." This is often in the negative (e.g., "time did not permit more discussion").
- Some object patterns
    permit + simple noun phrase (see In Context 1)
    permit + noun phrase + *to* verb (e.g., "The dean permitted Ray to start classes three weeks late")
- Often appears in the passive (see In Context 2)
- An authority *gives* or *grants* permission. You *receive* or *get* permission from the authority (e.g., "The dean gave Ray permission to begin classes three weeks late" OR "Ray got permission from the dean to begin classes three weeks late").
- Some fixed expressions; *time permitting*—"if there is enough time"; *weather permitting*—"if bad weather doesn't stop us"

allow

Form	Common Related Forms
Verb (transitive)	*allowance* (noun; countable when it means "something that is allowed"; uncountable when it means "the act of allowing") *allowable* (adjective meaning "able to be done because someone is likely to say it's okay") *allowed* (adjective meaning "able to be done because someone has already said it's okay")

In Context 1

The hospital allowed the police to interview the <u>victims</u> of the bombing.

In Context 2

The <u>raised</u> floor and wall <u>vents</u> allow free air <u>circulation</u>.

In Other Words

The hospital let the police speak to the people who had been hurt by bomb explosions.

In Other Words

An above-ground floor and some small openings in the walls make it possible for air to move freely in and out.

USAGE CLUES:

- Usable in most situations where *permit* works
- Some common subjects: laws, circumstances, conditions, people
- Common object patterns:
    allow noun phrase *to* verb (see In Context 1)
    allow noun phrase (see In Context 2)
- The noun *allowance* usually means (1) "an amount (especially of money) one is allowed to get" or (2) "an extra amount of consideration that is suitable under certain conditions" usually in the phrase *make allowance for* (e.g., "In planning the schedule we made allowance for the bad traffic").

Group 2. Adjectives that imply "allowing too much"

permissive

Form	Common Related Forms
Adjective	*permissiveness* (noun, uncountable)

In Context 1

Harvey's problems stem from his permissive <u>upbringing</u>.

In Context 2

President Fong <u>criticized</u> U.S. society for being permissive.

In Other Words

Harvey has problems now because there weren't enough controls on him when he was a child.

In Other Words

President Fong said that U.S. society is bad because people are allowed to do too many things.

lenient

Form	Common Related Forms
Adjective	*leniency* (noun, uncountable) *leniently* (adverbial)

In Context 1

Judge Abernathy was exceptionally lenient. He <u>sentenced</u> fewer <u>convicted</u> thieves to jail than any other judge in Minnesota.

In Other Words

Judge Abernathy was remarkably easy in his treatment of criminals. Of all the judges in Minnesota, he sent the fewest thieves to jail after the court found them guilty.

In Context 2

The finance department was lenient with late-paying customers, causing a severe <u>cash-flow</u> problem.

In Other Words

The finance department did not force customers to pay money they should have paid. This caused a big problem for the company, because the money it needed wasn't coming in on time.

To Help You Remember:

Comes from a Latin root meaning "soften" or "soothe." If you are lenient with someone, you relax your standards with him or her. Think about leaning, being relaxed.

Consolidation Exercises: Groups 1 and 2

8.1. Meanings and Connections. Next to each description, write *permit, allow, permissive,* or *lenient*—whichever best matches the description. Some of these items may be used more than once. Some may not be used at all.

_____ 1. comes from a Latin word meaning "soften"

_____ 2. works well in contexts about raising children

_____ 3. is part of fixed expressions about weather and time

_____ 4. works best in contexts about possible punishment

8.2. Collocations. Fill each blank with a word or phrase that goes well with the key vocabulary item. There are several possible answers to items 4, 5, and 6. *Hint:* Look at the Usage Clues and consider some of the additional vocabulary introduced in this section.

1. Principal Foster is too lenient _____ gang members operating at the school.

2. No one will be allowed _____ leave before noon.

3. Recently, the courts have _____ some leniency

_____ people arrested for possessing marijuana.

4. Preschool children with permissive _____ may

have trouble later on adapting to school.

5. We won't publish any photograph unless everyone in the picture _____

_____ us written permission.

6. Loose trade practices allow _____ .

8.3. Rephrasing. Using *permit, allow, permissive,* or *lenient,* rephrase each of
the following passages (write it in other words). You may change the form
of the item you use to fit the grammar of what you write. Change the words of
the original passage as much as necessary but don't change the meaning.

1. Improving our cash flow would make it possible for us to buy some new
computers.

2. The store's management lets the employees do whatever they want, and this
gives the store a bad image.

3. If you want to use a company car, you'll need to get your supervisor's signature
on a form.

4. We can let students make a few small changes in their research proposals.

5. Illegal photocopying continues because the courts have not punished people for
it severely enough.

6. The program will not accept a password if it contains any character other than a
letter or a number.

7. Rainwater drains well through soil that is loose and sandy.

Group 3. Nouns meaning "formal permission"

consent

Form	Common Related Forms
Noun (uncountable)	*consent* (verb, intransitive; often followed by *to*)

In Context 1

Reporters hoping to <u>interview</u> General Nawab waited for hours before he finally gave his consent to be interviewed.

In Other Words

Reporters who wanted to ask Nawab some questions waited a long time before he finally agreed to do it.

In Context 2

Baldridge's consent for several <u>cost-cutting</u> measures allowed us to balance the budget.

In Other Words

Because Baldridge said formally that she would let people take action to reduce expenses, we were able to avoid spending more money than we took in.

USAGE CLUES:

- Your consent can be for an activity that you will be part of (see In Context 1) or for an activity that you will not be a part of (see In Context 2).
- You *give* consent.
- The subject is a human or an organization.
- Can be followed by an infinitive (the *to* form of a verb) (see In Context 1)
- Can be followed by a *to* or *for* phrase describing what is being formally permitted (see In Context 2)
- An *of* phrase may name the person/group giving the consent (e.g., "You need the consent of the manager").
- Often useful in discussing something risky—business deals, etc.
- Some fixed phrases
  - *age of consent*—a point when someone is old enough to give formal agreement
  - *consenting adults*—people old enough to understand what they are doing and who are doing something freely

approval

Form	Common Related Forms
Noun (usually uncountable)	*approve* (verb, transitive/intransitive)

In Context 1

NATO gave approval for the <u>deployment</u> of <u>troops</u> near the airport.

In Other Words

NATO gave formal permission for soldiers to be put into positions near the airport.

In Context 2

The research cannot go ahead without approval from the FDA.

In Other Words

The research cannot continue unless the FDA (Food and Drug Administration, a governmental body) gives formal permission.

USAGE CLUES:

- *Approval* (unlike *consent*), works best when the person who gives approval for an action does not take part in the action. You approve the actions of others, not your own.
- If used in the plural (*approvals*) it means "several formal statements of permission" (e.g., "We got the necessary approvals").
- You *give* approval *for* something (see In Context 1) or *to* do something (e.g., "gave approval to deploy troops").
- Can be followed by a *from* phrase to name the person/group that agrees to an action (see In Context 2). A *by* phrase could do the same thing (e.g., "approval by the FDA").
- The person or group that gives approval must be in a position of authority.
- In this meaning ("give formal permission") the verb *approve* is followed directly by its object, NOT by an *of* phrase (e.g., "NATO approved the deployment of troops"). An *of* phrase would change the meaning of *approve* from a verb of permission to a verb of opinion.

As They Say

your John Hancock (or your John Henry)

your signature—an official signing of your name—to show your consent to or approval of something

> John Hancock was one of the signers of the Declaration of Independence, in which the colonies that eventually became the United States announced that they would no longer accept control by Great Britain. His signature became famous because it was large, clear, and easy to read.
>
> John Henry is an American folk hero. His name is sometimes used (by mistake) instead of Hancock's.
>
> *For example:*
>
> "Just put your John Hancock here, and we'll have a deal."

Group 4. Terms for being allowed NOT to do something

exempt

Form	Common Related Forms
Verb (transitive)	*exemption* (noun, countable) *exempt* (adjective)

In Context 1

The highway code exempts motorcyclists from paying <u>tolls</u>.

In Other Words

The law says it is okay for motorcyclists to *not* pay tolls. (A toll is an amount of money collected from the people who use the road.)

In Context 2

People whose religious beliefs forbid making war were exempted from military service.

In Other Words

If someone's religion did not allow fighting in a war, that person did not have to serve in the army or navy or air force.

USAGE CLUES:

- You exempt someone *from* an obligation or a duty.
- Common subjects of the active verb: laws, rules, systems
- Can occur as a regular passive (e.g., "They were exempted from"), but a pattern with *be* + adjective + *from* (e.g., "They were exempt from") is more likely.
- Do NOT use *exempt* if someone has started doing something and then gets permission to stop doing it. Use *excuse* instead.

excuse

Form	Common Related Forms
Verb (transitive)	*excuse* (noun, countable) *excusable* (adjective)

In Context 1

Harding asked to be excused from the meeting because he had a <u>headache</u>.

In Other Words

Harding asked someone to give him permission not to go to the meeting (or to leave a meeting that had already started) because his head hurt.

In Context 2

The need to develop economically does not excuse the government from <u>enforcing</u> environmental protection laws.

In Other Words

The country's need to grow economically does not make it okay for the government to let people break laws that would protect the natural environment.

USAGE CLUES:

- *Excuse* works better than *exempt* if the permission is spoken or not very formal.
- Use *excuse* (not *exempt*) if someone has started an activity and then gets permission to stop. (This is a possible meaning of In Context 1.)
- Common subjects: persons (see In Context 1; this implies that the person Harding asked would be the one to excuse him), conditions or behaviors (see In Context 2)
- You can "excuse yourself" from an event by asking others to let you out of it.

▢ Consolidation Exercises: Groups 3 and 4

8.4. Meanings and Connections. Next to each description, write *consent, approval, exempt,* or *excuse*—whichever best matches the description. Some of these items may be used more than once. Some may not be used at all.

_____ 1. means "give permission for someone not to do something"—but only to refer to an activity that has NOT already started

_____ 2. can mean "give permission for someone to stop doing an activity that he or she has already started"

_____ 3. You can give this for an action that you will take part in.

_____ 4. You can give this only for an action that someone else does.

8.5. Collocations. Fill each blank with a word or phrase that goes well with the key vocabulary item. *Hint:* Look at the Usage Clues and consider some of the additional vocabulary introduced in this section.

1. Kelsey's parents _____ the school their consent _____ include her in its gifted-child program.

2. U.S. citizens are exempt _____ visa requirements throughout most of East Asia.

3. I got the finance department's approval _____ a simplified reimbursement system.

4. Sherry Watkins excused herself _____ the training seminar after she got an emergency message on her pager.

5. If you want approval _____ build anything in this town, you have to talk to the city planner.

8.6. Rephrasing. Using *consent, approval, exempt,* or *excuse,* rephrase each of the following passages (write it in other words). You may change the form of the item you use to fit the grammar of what you write. Change the words of the original passage as much as necessary but don't change the meaning.

1. Any professional photographer knows that a picture can't be published unless the people who appear in it agree, in writing.

2. Very small businesses—those with fewer than 10 employees—don't have to follow the government's racial-diversity guidelines.

3. Our proposal to redesign the company's logo failed because the marketing manager wouldn't agree to let us do it.

4. The medical procedure was dangerous, but Mr. Harkins agreed to let the doctors perform it on him.

Group 5. Verbs meaning "make easier"

facilitate

Form	Common Related Forms
Verb (usually transitive)	*facilitator* (noun, countable) *facilitation* (noun, uncountable) *facilitative* (adjective)

In Context 1

You could facilitate the discussion by circulating your proposals before the meeting.

In Context 2

Opening the lid slightly will facilitate evaporation.

In Other Words

If you pass out copies of your proposals before the meeting, talking about them will be easier.

In Other Words

If you open the top of the container a little bit, the liquid will more easily turn to gas and go up into the air.

USAGE CLUES:

- Some common subjects: actions, conditions, processes, people
- The object has to be a process or an activity.
- Especially in the contexts of meetings, relationships, or discussions, *facilitate* is often used to mean "make a process work better without actually taking part in it" (e.g., "I'm here to facilitate, not to take a position").

ease

Form	Common Related Forms
Verb (transitive)	*easy* (adjective) *easily* (adverb) *ease* (noun, uncountable)

In Context 1

Proper financial planning can ease the process of <u>retirement</u>.

In Other Words

If you do a good job of planning what to do with your money, it can be easier for you when you stop having a job.

In Context 2

The World Bank hoped to ease the country's <u>transition</u> to a <u>market</u> <u>economy</u>.

In Other Words

The World Bank hoped to make it easier for the country to change to an economic system controlled mostly by the needs and wants of buyers and sellers, not mostly by the government.

USAGE CLUES:

- The subject can be an action or a process (see In Context 1) or a person or group (see In Context 2).
- The object is always a process or condition and often is a process that involves change.
- Some common objects: *transition* (see In Context 2), *pain, suffering*
- Works only in contexts where the object could involve difficulty
- Do not confuse with the intransitive/transitive verb *ease + into,* which means "enter/begin slowly."

Group 6. Verbs that mean "make easier" and involve metaphors about moving ahead

clear the way for

Form	Common Related Forms
Verb + noun phrase + preposition	None

In Context 1

Bob's <u>resignation</u> clears the way for Alice to become vice president.

In Context 2

The collapse of the central government cleared the way for rule by vicious gangs.

In Other Words

Bob left his job. Now there is nothing blocking Alice from becoming vice president.

In Other Words

After the nation's central government fell apart, it was easier for groups of violent people to take control.

USAGE CLUES:

- Some common subjects: events, actions, conditions. Can take a human subject, but the meaning changes somewhat, to "make changes that will permit a process to go forward."
- Can be followed by a simple noun phrase (see In Context 2) or by a noun phrase + infinitive (see In Context 1)
- Works well in writing about organizations, companies, politics, etc.
- Other variations on this phrase: *clear a path for, smooth the way for*

To Help You Remember:

Imagine a road (a way) blocked by fallen trees after a storm. If someone removes the trees, he or she clears the way.

remove obstacles to

Form	Common Related Forms
Verb + noun phrase + preposition	None

In Context 1

The Smith family's donation removed a huge obstacle to the university's expansion.

In Other Words

The Smith family gave some money to the university. This would make it easier for the university to expand. [The "obstacle" is understood to be "lack of money."]

In Context 2

By passing the English test, Martha removed the last obstacle to beginning her Ph.D. program.

In Other Words

Martha hadn't been able to start her studies for a doctoral degree, but passing the English test made it possible for her to start.

USAGE CLUES:

- *Obstacle* can also appear in the plural (*obstacles*).
- An adjective often appears before *obstacle* (see In Context 1 and 2).

- The subject is often a process or an action (see In Context 1).
- If the subject is a human, the sentence often contains a *by* phrase describing an action (see In Context 2).
- Variations on this phrase: *take away an obstacle to, remove a barrier to, remove a roadblock to*

To Help You Remember:

This creates an image similar to the one created by *clear the way for*—the image of a large thing blocking a path—but this phrase refers to the thing that blocks the path (not to the path itself).

Consolidation Exercises: Groups 5 and 6

8.7. Collocations. Fill each blank with a word or phrase that goes well with the key vocabulary item. There are several possible answers to each. *Hint:* Look at the Usage Clues and consider some of the additional vocabulary introduced in this section.

1. If you're thinking about moving to a new city, you can ease _____

   _____ by talking to other people who have lived there.

2. When Senator Beamer dropped out of the presidential race, that cleared the way

   for _____.

3. _____ facilitated government approval to sell our

   new product.

4. An agreement between the government and the two largest rebel groups re-

   moved a major obstacle to _____.

5. _____ cleared the way for the deployment of UN

   peacekeeping troops.

8.8. Rephrasing. Using *facilitate, ease, clear the way for,* or *remove an obstacle*
to rephrase each of the following passages (write it in other words). You
may change the form of the item you use to fit the grammar of what you write.
Change the words of the original passage as much as necessary but don't
change the meaning.

1. Draining the swamp made it easier for sugar farmers to move into the area.

2. Once the Harpers had divorced, it became easier for them to see the people they
really loved.

3. Increased funding for the police department made it easier to enforce laws
against drunk driving.

4. The dean exempted Andreas from the English language test, and this made it
easier for him to take a full load of English courses.

5. I don't want to take anyone's side in this argument, but I'm willing to help both
sides reach a settlement.

👁 Comprehensive Review Exercises

8.9. Matching. Next to each item in the left column, write the letter of the best description from the right column. Do not use any letter more than once.

_____ 1. permit/allow	a. works best in contexts of possible punishment
_____ 2. exempt	b. can be used when someone is permitted to stop doing an activity that has already started
_____ 3. excuse	
_____ 4. consent	c. works best in contexts of raising children or dealing with people who might cause trouble
_____ 5. approval	
_____ 6. facilitate	d. mentions a road or path
_____ 7. ease	e. You can give this for an action that you'll take part in.
_____ 8. permissive	
_____ 9. lenient	f. You can give this only for an action that someone else (not you) will perform.
_____ 10. clear the way for	
_____ 11. remove an obstacle to	g. Its object can be noun phrase + *to* + verb.

h. contains an image of a blocking thing or barrier

i. often has *transition* as its object

j. is especially useful to mean "help a relationship or discussion"

k. means "permitted to NOT do something"; works only if the action has not yet started

8.10. Fitting In. Choose the best word or phrase to complete each sentence. Write it in the blank.

Example: Because of the heavy rain, we had to <u>alter</u> our plans. (mutate, transform, alter)

1. This program doesn't _____ the user to exit quickly enough. (allow, ease, clear the way for)

2. Mr. Jefferson's students rarely do their homework, because he's so _____ _____ with people who don't do it. (permissive, lenient, exempt)

3. Installing brighter lightbulbs could _____ the process of repainting the hallway. (permit, clear the way for, facilitate)

4. The tax authorities _____ very poor people from

   paying taxes. (allow, remove an obstacle to, exempt)

5. After getting perfect scores for her first 3 presentations, Chandra was

   _____ from any further demonstrations.

   (exempt, excused, approved)

6. The county commission must give _____ for any

   new building project. (approval, excuse, allowance)

7. The law should not try to regulate sexual activity between

   _____ adults. (lenient, consenting, permitting)

8.11. Combinations and Collocations. Fill in each blank with a word or phrase that
fits well with the key vocabulary item. Many answers are possible for some
items.

1. The support of a parent can greatly ease a young person's _____

   _____ from childhood to adolescence.

2. The manager was too permissive _____ his sales

   staff, and now _____ .

3. After the security department cleared every visitor, the factory manager

   _____ her consent for _____

   _____ .

4. The law says that every car on the road has to be equipped with seat belts (one

   for each passenger), but it exempts _____ .

5. We need a better computer. The one we have now doesn't allow _____

   _____ .

6. _____ cleared the way for banks to begin selling

   securities, like stocks, bonds, and shares in mutual funds.

7. Unlike other companies, ours permits _____ .

Additional Vocabulary for Chapter 8

The additional words and phrases that have come up in the In Context examples in chapter 8 can be found in Appendix 1. (They are underlined when they occur in the In Context sections.) These terms are not fully explained, but you should be able to understand them from the contexts and brief explanations that are given. Do the exercises below to help solidify your understanding of these words and phrases.

8.12. Additional Vocabulary 1: Meanings. In each blank, write the letter of the meaning from column B that goes best with each vocabulary item in column A.

Column A

_____ 1. enforce
_____ 2. market economy
_____ 3. circulation
_____ 4. personal
_____ 5. toll
_____ 6. to sentence
_____ 7. resignation
_____ 8. retirement
_____ 9. evaporation
_____ 10. upbringing
_____ 11. cash flow

Column B

a. being cared for and trained during childhood
b. leaving a specific job (by choice, not because of being fired)
c. leaving an entire kind of work because of age or because you don't want to do that kind of work anymore
d. a process in which a liquid becomes a gas
e. money you pay in order to use something (like a road)
f. make sure a law or rule is being obeyed
g. the movement of money into and out of a business
h. related to one person; private
i. an economic system influenced mostly by the demands of buyers and sellers (not government control)
j. to give a punishment to someone convicted of a crime
k. going through; moving around in a circular way

8.13. Additional Vocabulary 2: Fitting into Sentences. Fill each blank on page 186 with one of the additional vocabulary items from the list below. You may have to change the form of the item to fit the grammar of the sentence. Do not use any item more than once. Some items will not be used at all.

cash flow	deployment	sentence
convicted	headache	troops
criticized	interview	vent
cut costs	raised	victim

1. If we want to stay within our budget, we have two choices—bringing in more money or _____.

2. After we narrow our list of job candidates to three or four people, we can call them for _____.

3. The builders always install a(n) _____ in the bathroom to remove moisture after a shower.

4. You don't look like you're feeling well. Do you have a(n) _____ _____?

5. Angry parents _____ the school administration for letting some students come to school with guns or other weapons.

6. In some states a _____ criminal cannot get a driver's license.

7. The sight of American soldiers being dragged through the streets of Mogadishu made the U.S. government afraid to _____ troops overseas in later conflicts.

8. American prisons became crowded after judges began _____ _____ people to long terms for minor drug offenses.

⫴ **Writing Projects**

8.14. Writing Projects. The following are some suggestions for writing projects that will allow you to use the key vocabulary and some of the additional vocabulary. Each of the topics could be lightly covered in an essay of 500–600 words or more thoroughly in a paper of 1,500–2,000 words. To write information-packed longer papers (especially about topics 4, 5, and 6) you should do some research in the library and/or on the Internet.

1. Are there any rules in your university or school or workplace that are too restrictive—that keep you from doing what you think you should be able to do? Use the key vocabulary to describe what your school or employer should let you do.

2. When you were a child, what did your parents allow you to do? Use the key vocabulary to describe this.

3. Most people have received valuable help from another person (or group) at some point in their lives. Think of some factor in your life—the support of your parents, extra attention from a teacher, some exceptional help from a friend, etc.—that has allowed you to enjoy the success you have had so far. This topic is perhaps more suitable for a short essay than for a long one. If you do choose a longer format for this essay, make an extra effort to be very detailed in your analysis and description.

4. Think of a conflict or an international disagreement that had lasted a long time but was finally resolved—perhaps peacefully, perhaps after a struggle. Some examples from recent history include

    the end of the Cold War between the Soviet Union and the United States
    the end of apartheid in South Africa
    the return of Hong Kong and Macao to China after years of rule by
        European powers

    These are just a few examples. You can certainly think of other such resolved conflicts. Choose one (from the list above or from your own knowledge) and write an essay discussing what might have changed to bring about this final resolution. Focus on the factors that permitted this resolution or made it easier.

5. Alternatively, choose a conflict that has been going on for a long time and is still going on. Write an essay discussing some factors that, if they occurred, could possibly make a resolution of this conflict easier.

6. As the human population of the world grew rapidly during the 1950s and 1960s, it seemed that soon the world would run out of food. Many writers of that time predicted disasters in which millions of people would die each year from starvation. The population of the world is now greater than 6 billion (and will probably reach 8 billion by the year 2025), but widespread starvation has not yet occurred. (Many people have died of hunger, but such famine has been

localized rather than widespread.) On this topic of a possible food crisis for the world's growing population, choose one of the following options.

(a) Write an essay in which you discuss why the world has, in general, been able to feed itself despite an ever-rising population. This should be an essay mostly about the past and the present, not a prediction of the future. Some of the topics you might want to research are as follows: the green revolution, agricultural biotechnology, food preservation, and "factory farms." Use the key vocabulary as much as possible to describe how certain factors have made it easier for the world to produce and distribute food.

(b) Write an essay in which you discuss whether the world's general success at feeding itself is likely to continue. In this essay, you should look at the past and the present as indicators of the future. Be sure to have solid evidence for the predictions you make about the future. Use the key vocabulary as much as possible to describe how certain factors might make it easier—or harder—for the world to produce and distribute food. You might also want to look at the vocabulary in chapter 9, "Stopping, Preventing," and use some of those terms in your essay.

Chapter 9   **Stopping, Preventing**

This vocabulary may be useful when:

You want to describe how certain factors make something impossible or difficult. See also chapter 2, "Excluding, Not Being Part Of."

Key Vocabulary

Group 1	Group 2	Group 3	Group 4	Group 5
halt	restrict	forbid	prevent	hinder
cease	restrain	deny	forestall	block
suspend				deter

⚙ Exploring the Vocabulary

Group 1. Stopping completely

halt

Form	Common Related Forms
Verb (transitive/intransitive)	*halt* (noun, countable but usually singular)
	NOT in this meaning: *halting*

In Context 1

The new law required American companies to halt exports of computer technology to the republic of Briggandia.

In Other Words

The new law said that American companies could no longer ship computer equipment or plans to the republic of Briggandia.

In Context 2

Work on the new <u>mall</u> halted after <u>interest rates</u> rose.

In Other Words

Work on the new very large shopping center stopped after it became more expensive to borrow money.

USAGE CLUES:

- Has a sense of finality and firmness—that the stop is necessary
- In the transitive sense (see In Context 1), it works well when someone has ordered or commanded that something must stop.
- Some common subjects of the transitive form: laws, government officials or divisions, difficult circumstances or obstacles
- Some common objects of the transitive form: *war, fighting, campaign, production,* words for processes or events
- Some common subjects of the intransitive form: processes, events
- The noun *halt* appears in a large number of standard phrases.
    transitive verb phrases (meaning "make X stop"): *bring X to a halt, call a halt to X*
    intransitive verb phrases (meaning "stop"): *come to a halt, grind to a halt* ("go slower and slower until eventually stopping, usually while experiencing some difficulty"), *coast/roll to a halt* ("come to a smooth stop, usually after a force stops working on something"), *screech to a halt* ("stop very suddenly")

cease

Form	Common Related Forms
Verb (transitive/ intransitive)	*cessation* (noun, uncountable) *ceaseless* (adjective)

In Context 1

The storm <u>raged</u> on day after day, and we began to wonder whether the rain would ever cease.

In Context 2

As wages in the private sector rose, government employment ceased to attract many <u>talented</u> young people.

In Other Words

The storm continued with violent force day after day, and we started to wonder whether the rain would ever stop.

In Other Words

As jobs with private companies paid more and more money, jobs with the government stopped drawing in many young people who were smart and had the ability to do good work.

USAGE CLUES:

- Has a slightly formal or old-fashioned tone but is still relatively common
- Common subjects for the intransitive form (see In Context 1): processes, events, conditions
- The subject of the transitive form is usually the actor in a process that stops. See In Context 2, where *government employment* is the actor in the process of *attracting*—the process that stops.
- The object of the transitive verb is always a process or an event. This object is usually in the form of an infinitive (the *to* form of a verb; see In Context 2) or a gerund (the *-ing* form of a verb; e.g., "government employment ceased attracting young people").
- *BE CAREFUL:* The transitive form can sometimes (but less commonly) have an object that is a simple noun phrase, often including a possessive (e.g., "the bees ceased their dance"). However, not every noun works in this pattern, and choosing such nouns properly requires a very good sense of English style. It is safer to use an object that is an infinitive or a gerund.
- The subject of the intransitive form is the thing that stops.
- *Cease* occurs in many set phrases, including *cease-fire* ("a temporary end to fighting"), *cease and desist* (a formal and emphatic way of saying "stop"), *it never ceases to amaze me* ("it always seems very unusual to me").

suspend

Form	Common Related Forms
Verb (transitive)	*suspension* (noun, uncountable) *suspended* (adjective) NOT in this meaning: *suspense, suspenseful*

In Context 1

To encourage people to return books, the library declared an amnesty period, during which it suspended fines for overdue materials.

In Context 2

Last November, classes were suspended indefinitely because of campus unrest.

In Other Words

To get people to return books, the library declared an amnesty period—a time when it temporarily stopped requiring people to pay fines (money they must pay as a punishment) for materials that were not returned on time.

In Other Words

Last November, classes stopped being held because there were protests and occasional fights on the property of the college—and this stoppage was indefinite (no one knew how long it would last).

USAGE CLUES:

- To suspend something is to stop it temporarily, even though you expect it to resume again after a while.
- When the verb is active (see In Context 1), the subject is usually a person or an organization, but it could also be a factor that causes a suspension (e.g., "Campus unrest suspended classes indefinitely").
- Some common objects: *law, rule, judgment, sentence* (a legal punishment), terms for processes, actions, conditions, events, or meetings
- Very often passive (see In Context 2)
- Some common expressions with *suspend: suspended sentence* (a punishment that has been declared but that won't be enforced), *suspend something indefinitely* (stop it for a period of time but without knowing how long that period will be; see In Context 2)

As They Say

(willing) suspension of disbelief

a willingness to accept something (especially in a book, a movie, or other entertainment) as believable, even though you know it is not true

For example:

"Science fiction is more fiction than science, requiring even more suspension of disbelief than most other forms of fiction."

This means "Science fiction is far more like a story than it is like true science, and it requires an exceptional effort by the audience to pretend that unbelievable things are true."

The term *willing suspension of disbelief* is a quote from the British poet Samuel Taylor Coleridge. Originally used to refer to poetry, it now most often refers to the way audiences approach movies or television shows (and, less often, literature). If a movie audience willingly suspends disbelief, they are willing to accept characters, settings, or plots that are not very realistic so the movie can be enjoyed without too much criticism.

◨ Consolidation Exercises: Group 1

9.1. Collocations. Fill each blank with a word or phrase that goes well with the key vocabulary item. There are several possible answers to items 1, 3, 4, and 5. *Hint:* Look at the Usage Clues and consider some of the additional vocabulary introduced in this section.

1. As fuel became harder to get, the nation's industry slowly _____

   _____ to a halt.

2. The bank suspended its lending operations _____

   six weeks while investigators looked into alleged financial irregularities.

3. After trying for several months to hire a new public relations manager, we

   ceased _____ for someone and simply closed our

   public relations department.

4. _____ halted the practice of allowing businesses

   to "donate" money to local politicians.

5. Every time I think there's no way to finish a project, he finds a way to do it. It

   never ceases to _____ .

9.2. Rephrasing. Using *halt, cease,* or *suspend,* rephrase each of the following passages (write it in other words). You may change the form of the item you use to fit the grammar of what you write. Change the words of the original passage as much as necessary but don't change the meaning.

1. An order from the court said that the company had to stop selling the insecticide known as Fortidonic because it had been connected to serious illnesses in humans.

2. In the condition known as Herberger's disease, the pituitary gland stops producing hormones necessary for normal development of the human body.

3. Relations between the two companies became so bad that they stopped sharing information with each other about new developments in the market.

4. The Delaney family stopped donating money to St. Aikman's College for a while because they disliked the college's president.

Group 2. Placing limits on something

restrict

Form	Common Related Forms
Verb (transitive)	*restriction* (noun, countable/uncountable) *restrictive* (adjective) *restricted* (adjective)

In Context 1

Though he wasn't formally under arrest, General Bosevich's movements were restricted to a 2-square-kilometer area near his party headquarters.

In Other Words

Although he was not actually being held by the police, General Bosevich was allowed to move around only within an area of about 2 square kilometers near the place where his party had its offices.

In Context 2

Rising fuel prices have restricted the growth of FlightComp Airlines during the past few years.

In Other Words

Higher prices for fuel have kept FlightComp Airlines from growing as fast as it otherwise would have grown during the past few years.

USAGE CLUES:

- Often followed by a *to* phrase naming an area, a part, or a small group that IS allowed (see In Context 1)
- When the verb is active (see In Context 2), the subject is a person or thing that creates limits. The object is the thing that is limited.
- Some common objects of the active verb: ranges, movements, amounts, actions, power, behavior
- The active verb is often reflexive, so that its object is a *-self* pronoun, followed by a *to* phrase (e.g., "I restrict myself to two drinks per night").
- Very often in the passive. The subject of the passive verb is the thing that is limited (see In Context 1).

To Help You Remember:

Comes from a Latin root that means "tie up" or "bind." In fact, the English word *string* (meaning "a long, thin piece of material that is used in tying things") comes from the same word family.

restrain

Form	Common Related Forms
Verb (transitive)	*restraint* (noun, countable/uncountable) *restrained* (adjective)

In Context 1

The seawall at Port Burke can control ordinary waves but could not restrain the fury of a <u>tidal wave</u>.

In Other Words

The seawall (a wall stretching out from the shore into the water) at Port Burke can keep ordinary waves from causing trouble but would not be able to limit the destructive force of a tidal wave. (A tidal wave is a large wave caused by an earthquake, a volcanic eruption, or some other large force.)

In Context 2

Only a direct <u>appeal</u> from the religious leaders restrained people in their violent protests against the president.

In Other Words

The people who were demonstrating against the president were held back from becoming more violent only after the religious leaders made a direct request.

USAGE CLUES:

- Has a sense of "holding back"
- Very similar in meaning to *restrict,* but *restrain* fits best into contexts of great force that is being kept under control.
- Some common subjects: people, organizations, laws, structures or instruments that commonly hold things back (e.g., ropes, barriers), statements
- The object is usually a force or someone who can act forcefully.
- The object is often followed by an *in* phrase naming the action that is limited (see In Context 2).
- Like *restrict,* is often used reflexively—with a *-self* pronoun as its object (e.g., "I felt like crying, but I restrained myself")

Group 3. Not giving permission

forbid

Form	Common Related Forms
Verb (transitive/ditransitive) irregular past: *forbade* irregular past participle: *forbidden*	*forbidden* (adjective) NOT in this meaning: *forbidding* (adjective)

In Context 1

The law in Forgonia forbids marriage between people of different religions.

In Other Words

The law in Forgonia says that people may not get married if they belong to different religions.

In Context 2

Throughout the peace talks there was a news blackout, during which members of the delegations were forbidden to talk to the press.

In Other Words

While officials were trying to agree about a way to stop a war, the people on each side of these talks were not allowed to speak to reporters from newspapers or other media.

USAGE CLUES:

- Works best in the context of an official statement

When the verb is active (see In Context 1)

- Common subjects: laws, rules, governmental bodies, people in positions of authority
- Common object patterns
    simple noun phrase (see In Context 1)
    gerund (the *-ing* form of a verb) (e.g., "The Park Board forbids swimming after Labor Day")
    noun phrase + infinitive (the *to* form of a verb) (e.g., "The law forbids people of different religions to marry")

Is very often *passive* (see In Context 2)

- When the verb is passive and followed by an infinitive (see In Context 2), the subject is a person or thing that may not perform an action.
- When the verb is passive and NOT followed by an infinitive, the subject is an action that is not permitted (e.g., "Talking to the press was forbidden").
- Can also be a ditransitive verb—followed by both an indirect object and a direct object (e.g., "His parents forbade him any contact with lower-class students"). The indirect object names someone who is not allowed to have something. The direct object names the thing someone may not get. However, this ditransitive usage sounds old fashioned and very formal.

 To Help You Remember:

Is a very old English word, coming from Germanic roots meaning "proclaim that something is not allowed." Its most common modern context—referring to official statements—keeps that meaning of a proclamation (an official announcement).

deny

Form	Common Related Forms
Verb (transitive/ditransitive)	*denial* (noun, uncountable)

In Context 1

(active) The department <u>chair</u> denied our request for more research funding.
(passive) Our request for more research funding was denied by the department chair.

In Other Words

The person in charge of our department said that we could not have more money to conduct our research.

In Context 2

(active) The government denied foreign researchers access to files describing weapons technology.
(passive 1) Foreign researchers were denied access to files describing weapons technology.
(passive 2) Access to files describing weapons technology was denied to foreign researchers.

In Other Words

Researchers from other countries were not allowed to get into files that described ways of making weapons.

USAGE CLUES:

- Works best in contexts where someone has tried to get a thing—or at least wants to get it—but is not allowed to have it
- Can be a simple transitive verb, with a simple direct object (see In Context 1). When the verb is in this form, the subject is usually a person or an organization in a position of authority, and the object is almost always a noun for a kind of request (*request, petition, application, appeal,* etc.).
- Is often passive
- Is also common as a ditransitive verb—followed by both an indirect object and a direct object (see In Context 2). The indirect object names someone who is not allowed to have something. The direct object names the thing someone may not get.
- The ditransitive verb is often passive. The subject of this passive is usually a person (the indirect object in the active construction;—see In Context 2, passive 1). Less often, the subject of the passive can be the thing that is not given (see In Context 2, passive 2).
- *BE CAREFUL:* Do not confuse this with another meaning of *deny*—"say that something is not true."

Consolidation Exercises: Groups 2 and 3

9.3. Collocations. Fill each blank with a word or phrase that goes well with the key vocabulary item. There are several possible answers to items 3, 4, and 5. *Hint:* Look at the Usage Clues and consider some of the additional vocabulary introduced in this section.

1. Even though I was very angry, I restrained _____ and didn't say what I was thinking.

2. People on Dr. Tollefson's diet try to lose weight by restricting themselves _____ two medium-size meals each day.

3. Because the U.S. government denied _____ visas, several British skiers were unable to take part in the winter Olympics.

4. Instructors at Delta State University are forbidden _____ _____.

5. Many governments have found that, in the age of the Internet, it is almost impossible to restrain _____.

9.4. Rephrasing. Using *restrict, restrain, forbid,* or *deny,* rephrase each of the following passages (write it in other words). You may change the form of the item you use to fit the grammar of what you write. Change the words of the original passage as much as necessary but don't change the meaning. In some cases (especially items 3 and 4), you may be able to use more than one of the key words in your rephrased passage.

1. The law says that if a judge owns shares of a company, that judge cannot be in charge of any court case involving that company.

2. After Mr. Harcourt was arrested, the police did not allow him to use a telephone to call his lawyer right away.

3. Most people who take tours of the White House are allowed to see only certain public or ceremonial rooms. They are not allowed to see any of the places where the president or presidential aides are actually working.

4. American law is very strict about "sexual harassment," and a corporate disaster can occur if one employee attempts to develop a romantic relationship with another. If an employee feels any desire to strike up a romance with another, this desire should be kept under control.

Group 4. Stopping something before it starts

prevent

Form	Common Related Forms
Verb (transitive)	*prevention* (noun, uncountable) *preventive* (adjective)

In Context 1

Wise decisions by the director of the Central Bank prevented the economy from collapsing.

In Context 2

A <u>vaccine</u> prevents disease, whereas a therapy treats disease that has already <u>gotten under way</u>.

In Other Words

Good decisions by the person in charge of the Central Bank stopped the economy from falling apart.

In Other Words

A vaccine makes it difficult for a disease to infect a person, but a therapy deals with a disease that has already started. (A vaccine is a weak form of a disease—or of some related disease—that is given to a person to build up immunity to serious infection.)

USAGE CLUES:

- An extremely useful, versatile verb for this meaning. It is neutral in tone and can work in nearly any context.
- Often appears in the passive, and this passive is often followed by a *from* phrase (e.g., "We were prevented from entering the building").
- The object of the active verb is usually a process, an event, or a condition. Some common ones are *crime, disease, outbreak, loss,* and *recurrence.*
- Some common object patterns for the active verb
    prevent someone/something *from* verb-*ing* (see In Context 1)
    prevent + simple noun phrase (see In Context 2)

prevent someone's/something's noun phrase (e.g., "They could not prevent Alanson's defeat in the election")

- The noun *prevention* often occurs in compounds with other nouns for undesirable things (e.g., *disease prevention, crime prevention, suicide prevention, decay prevention, fire prevention*).

As They Say

An ounce of prevention is worth a pound of cure.

This means "It's far better to make sure a problem doesn't occur than to correct it afterward."

For example:

A: We should put a cover over that sofa before the party to protect it from spills.
B: An ounce of prevention is worth a pound of cure.

Speaker B is agreeing with Speaker A and is saying that the sofa won't have to be cleaned later if they cover it now.

forestall

Form	Common Related Forms
Verb (transitive)	None

In Context 1

The sale of our shares in Condorco was forestalled by legal action against the company.

In Context 2

Swift action by the prime minister forestalled the failure of the nation's fuel-distribution system.

In Other Words

We had hoped to sell our shares in Condorco, but we couldn't because the company was being taken to court.

In Other Words

Because the prime minister acted quickly, the nation's system for getting fuel to many different places did not fall apart.

USAGE CLUES:

- Has a somewhat formal tone
- Common subjects: terms for people, actions, conditions
- Common objects: terms for attacks or wars, disasters (see In Context 2), events, processes, actions (see In Context 1), conditions
- Is often passive (see In Context 1)

 To Help You Remember:

Comes from an old English word that often meant "to get into a position ahead of a traveler, so you can jump out and attack the traveler before he or she reaches a destination." If you forestall an action, it is like acting quickly to stop the action before it can proceed very far.

Group 5. Slowing down a process or making it difficult

hinder

Form	Common Related Forms
Verb (transitive)	*hindrance* (noun, countable/uncountable)

In Context 1

Opposition from religious groups hindered the passage of laws allowing the sale of alcohol in grocery stores.

In Context 2

Repeated equipment failures and <u>power outages</u> hindered Gordon in his research.

In Other Words

Because religious groups didn't like laws that would permit the sale of alcoholic drinks in most food stores, passing such laws became more difficult.

In Other Words

Gordon's research was slower and more difficult because his machines kept breaking down and he often had no electrical power.

USAGE CLUES:

- Works well when a process is slowed down or made more difficult—but not very seriously. The process is likely to continue even though it has been slowed down.
- Some common subjects: conditions, events, undesirable factors, people, rules
- When the object is a thing (not a person or group), it is usually something good that a person is trying to achieve. Some common objects: *progress, pursuit, effort, development, growth,* other terms for processes or activities (see In Context 1).
- The object can also be a person or group (see In Context 2).
- If the object is a person or group, it is often followed by an *in* phrase naming the process that is slowed down (see In Context 2).
- Less commonly, an object that is a person or a group might be followed by a *from* phrase naming some process of achievement (e.g., "The weather hindered him from completing his around-the-world balloon trip").

block

Form	Common Related Forms
Verb (transitive)	*block* (noun, countable)

In Context 1

After blocking Princess Maria's rise to the throne, Queen Filomina had her imprisoned on the island of Servona.

In Context 2

Aspirin helps relieve pain because it blocks the production of chemicals called prostaglandins, which the body would otherwise produce in great amounts after an injury.

In Other Words

After making sure that Princess Maria did not become queen, Filomina (who did become queen) put Maria in a jail on the island of Servona.

In Other Words

Aspirin (a drug that contains salicylic acid; $C_7H_6O_3$) helps reduce pain levels because it stops the body's normal production of a hormonelike chemical called prostaglandin. Without aspirin, the body would normally make a lot of prostaglandin after a person got hurt.

USAGE CLUES:

- If a process is blocked, it may move ahead again later (if the barrier is removed; see In Context 2, where the production of prostaglandin could occur again after aspirin is no longer in a person's system), or it may be stopped permanently (see In Context 1).
- Often used in medical or chemical contexts (see In Context 2) or political contexts
- Some common objects: *path, attempt, process, progress, pain,* other terms for processes, actors in processes, or routes that someone may travel
- The object may also be a person or group. In these cases, it's often followed by a *from* phrase or an *in* phrase naming the action that the person or group is kept from pursuing (e.g., "Johnson was blocked from reforming the department" OR "Johnson was blocked in his efforts to reform the department").

deter

Form	Common Related Forms
Verb (transitive)	*deterrence* (noun, uncountable) *deterrent* (noun, countable)

In Context 1

An <u>outcry</u> from environmentalists deterred TreeHarvester, Inc., from cutting down 200-year-old cedars.

In Context 2

An increase in the number of shore <u>patrols</u> deterred <u>drug trafficking</u> along the Louisiana coast.

In Other Words

A strong, loud protest from environmentalists made TreeHarvester, Inc., decide not to cut down some very old cedar trees.

In Other Words

Because more police were traveling along the Louisiana coast, looking for illegal activity, there was less smuggling of illegal drugs into the country in that area.

USAGE CLUES:

- Works well in contexts of discouraging an action—slowing it or stopping it by making someone not want to do it
- The object can be either a person/group (see In Context 1) or an activity (see In Context 2).
- If the object is a person, it is often followed by a prepositional phrase naming the action that the person is discouraged from doing. This could be
    - a *from* phrase, often including a gerund (the *-ing* form of a verb); see In Context 1
    - an *in* phrase, often including a possessive + noun (e.g., "deterred Tree-Harvester, Inc., in their plan to cut down 200-year-old cedars")
- *Deterrence* and *deterrent* are common in a military sense—especially in relation to nuclear weapons. A nuclear deterrent is a supply of nuclear weapons that will discourage other countries from attacking.

 To Help You Remember:

Comes from a Latin root meaning "to scare away." (The English word *terror* ["fear"] has similar ancestors.) If you deter someone, you make that person think that something bad will happen if he or she carries out an action—you "scare" the person out of doing it.

⬚ Consolidation Exercises: Groups 4 and 5

9.5. Collocations. Fill each blank with a word or phrase that goes well with the key term (or a related form). There are several possible answers to items 3, 4, and 5. *Hint:* Look at the Usage Clues and consider some of the additional vocabulary introduced in this section.

1. Strong winds and snow hindered rescuers _____
   their attempt to reach survivors of the plane crash.

2. The fact that he was not born in the United States prevented Secretary of State
   Fiorello _____ becoming president.

3. Even for people who tend to put on weight easily, a healthy diet and regular
   exercise can forestall _____.

4. The president wanted to protect refugees fleeing the civil war in Fulona, but
   fears of public opposition deterred _____.

5. The doctors were able to block _____ by giving
   the patient a combination of aspirin and other drugs.

9.6. Rephrasing. Use one of the key terms (*prevent, forestall, hinder, block, deter*) to rephrase each of the following statements. You may change the form of the key term if necessary. Do not change the meaning of the original statement.

1. General Fletcher tried to take over the government, but troops loyal to the president stopped this attempt.

2. A lack of training in statistics makes it hard for many managers to do their jobs correctly.

3. Some signs of aging—such as wrinkled skin and a loss of muscle mass—did not appear in laboratory rats if the researchers put large amounts of sunflower oil into the rats' food.

4. According to one line of reasoning, people will not commit certain more serious crimes if they know that the penalty for such crimes is death.

5. After hearing an emotional appeal on television from the mother of one hostage, the kidnappers decided not to kill the people they had been holding.

◉ Comprehensive Review Exercises

9.7. Meanings and Connections. Next to each item in the left column, write the letter of the best meaning or description from the right column. Do not use any letter more than once.

____ 1. block

____ 2. cease

____ 3. deny

____ 4. deter

____ 5. forbid

____ 6. forestall

____ 7. halt

____ 8. hinder

____ 9. prevent

____ 10. restrain

____ 11. restrict

____ 12. suspend

a. The object can be a simple noun phrase, but these are hard to choose; it's better to use an object that is an infinitive or a gerund.

b. Means "say something is not allowed"; the subject is always a rule or a person/group in a position of authority.

c. The object is almost always a force or something/someone able to act forcefully.

d. Means "make more difficult" but doesn't mean "stop forever"; the process could eventually be completed.

e. Means "stop for a while" but doesn't necessarily mean "stop entirely"; the process could eventually start again.

f. is a versatile term for "before something can start, make sure it won't happen"; its object is often followed by a *from* phrase naming the action that won't occur

g. means, "keep something from happening by causing someone to think that it would be a bad idea"; comes from a root meaning "scare away"

h. The noun form occurs in such phrases as *come to a . . . , grind to a . . . ,* or *screech to a . . . .*

i. Its object is often followed by a *to* phrase naming a small area or thing that IS allowed.

j. Sounds somewhat formal; the object is usually a war or a disaster.

k. Creates an image of a large obstacle in a road; often used in medical, chemical, or political contexts

l. can take an indirect AND a direct object

9.8. Meanings and Connections. Name some things that

can be restricted_____

can be suspended _____

cannot be prevented _____

9.9. Usage Practice. Fill each blank in the left column with an item from the right column. Do not use any item more than once.

1. The war ended in a _____ -fire.   restricted

2. You may not leave. Permission _____ .   restraint

3. You're angry, but stay calm. Show some _____ .   prevent

4. A good sunscreen will _____ harmful radiation.   cease

5. Eating properly helps _____ disease.   block

6. Stay out. This is a _____ area.   denied

9.10. Fitting In. Choose the best word or phrase to complete each sentence. Write it in the blank.

> *Example:* Because of the heavy rain, we had to <u>alter</u> our plans. (mutate, transform, alter)

1. International copyright law _____ photo-copying and distributing somebody else's work without the permission of the copyright holder. (denies, halts, forbids)

2. Developing a strong, trusting relationship with your children in their preteen years can _____ many of the communication problems usually associated with adolescence. (forestall, restrain, suspend)

3. The influenza vaccine didn't totally wipe out the disease, but it did _____ thousands of people from getting sick. (prevent, forestall, hinder)

4. According to our department's policies, access to information about research budgets is _____ to full-time faculty and administrators. No one else is allowed to see those figures. (blocked, restricted, restrained)

5. Funding for the National Poetic Arts Program was _____ because of World War II but was reestablished in the early 1950s. (suspended, hindered, denied)

6. After the Bloombergs divorced, the shouting and bickering coming from 5843 Nearton Lane finally _____. (ceased, forestalled, restrained)

7. I have a hard time imagining a controlled-fusion energy system, something that could _____ the violence of an H-bomb explosion and channel all that force into the illumination of lightbulbs and the running of radios. (restrict, restrain, block)

8. The drugs known as serotonin-reuptake inhibitors work by _____ _____ the natural breakdown of a chemical called serotonin. With higher levels of serotonin in their bodies, people are less likely to behave in an impulsive, unpredictable way. (denying, blocking, deterring)

9. The game was great. Johnson _____ Hollister any chance to get into the end zone. (forbade, halted, denied)

10. Prior to 1990, most new albums of recorded music were available on large vinyl disks, but the great popularity of CDs eventually brought the routine issuance of vinyl versions to a(n) _____. (suspension, deterrent, halt)

9.11. Combinations and Collocations. Fill in each blank with a word or phrase that fits well with the key vocabulary item. Many answers are possible for items 3, 5, 6, and 7. *Hint:* Look at the Usage Clues and consider some of the additional vocabulary introduced in this section.

1. Fearing that Frederickson's careless comments to the press might eventually get the company in trouble, the managing director ordered her to cease and _____.

2. You can't get to the island by boat now, because all ferry service has been suspended _____ next April.

3. As Quigley crept toward the gate, he heard a guard _____ _____, "Halt!"

4. Reports that several people had fallen ill while traveling through Nepal

   deterred the Upton University group _____

   _____ taking a side trip to Kathmandu.

5. In order to prevent _____,

   you should always carefully put out your campfire and bury any hot embers

   under at least one inch of soil.

6. While training for the Olympics, the gymnasts were restricted _____

   _____.

7. The police announced that the protesters were forbidden _____

   _____, but such a small number of police officers

   could not block _____.

8. Diplomats from the two countries negotiated long into the night, but they were

   unable to forestall _____.

9. Unfortunately, in the United States in the 1950s, a person's race or color

   commonly denied _____.

Additional Vocabulary for Chapter 9

The additional words and phrases that have come up in the In Context examples in chapter 9 can be found in Appendix 1. (They are underlined when they occur in the In Context sections.) These terms are not fully explained, but you should be able to understand them from the contexts and brief explanations that are given. Do the exercises below to help solidify your understanding of these words and phrases.

9.12. Additional Vocabulary 1: Meanings. In each blank, write the letter of the meaning from column B that goes best with each vocabulary item in column A.

Column A

_____ 1. amnesty
_____ 2. aspirin
_____ 3. chair
_____ 4. fine
_____ 5. indefinitely
_____ 6. injury
_____ 7. mall
_____ 8. overdue
_____ 9. rage
_____ 10. swift
_____ 11. tidal wave
_____ 12. vaccine

Column B

a. not done on time; handed in late
b. the head of a department in a university
c. extreme, violent anger
d. being hurt
e. a medical treatment that builds up immunity to a disease
f. medicine that can relieve pain
g. money you have to pay as a penalty or punishment
h. a very large surge of water, often caused by an underwater earthquake or explosion
i. quick
j. for an undefined period of time
k. a large, indoor shopping area
l. a declaration that someone will not be punished for something he or she did wrong

9.13. Additional Vocabulary 2: Fitting into Sentences. Fill each blank with one of the additional vocabulary items from the list below. You may have to change the form of an item to fit the grammar of the sentence. Do not use any item more than once. Some items will not be used at all.

appeal	get under way	power outage
aspirin	imprison	rage
chair	indefinitely	talented
collapse	interest rate	vaccine
drug trafficking	patrol	

1. In court, Barnard claimed that the two kilograms of marijuana found in his car had been for his own use, but the jury didn't believe him and convicted him of _____.

2. Giselle's doctors advised her not to take _____
   to relieve headache pain. They recommended other analgesics—like
   acetaminophen or ibuprofen—instead.

3. Telford's home mortgage was large ($220,000), so a small increase in the
   _____ from 8.15 % to 8.42% raised her
   monthly house payment by a significant amount.

4. The graduation ceremony was scheduled for 8:00, but it was 8:45 before it
   finally _____.

5. If you try to drive a truck over that old wooden bridge, it will _____
   _____.

6. When you look at Charles Greaver now—drunk, depressed, in and out of jail
   on a daily basis—it's hard to remember that he was once one of America's
   most _____ pianists.

7. While on _____ in a remote area of Nevada,
   federal law-enforcement officers discovered a small shed that had obviously
   been used in making amphetamines and other illegal drugs.

8. I always keep a flashlight near my bed in case there's a _____
   _____ and I need some light in order to move throughout the
   house.

9. The president of the Blood Bank of America made an _____
   _____ over national television in which she asked for blood
   donations to correct a severe shortage of plasma in the nation's hospitals.

10. After being sentenced to life in prison, the convicted murderer flew into a
    _____ and tried to attack the judge and jury.

‖⫝̸ Writing Projects

9.14. Writing Projects. The following are some suggestions for writing projects that will allow you to use the key vocabulary and some of the additional vocabulary. Each of the topics could be lightly covered in an essay of 500–600 words or more thoroughly in a paper of 1,500–2,000 words. To write information-packed longer papers (especially about topics 2, 3, and 4) you should do some research in the library and/or on the Internet.

1. Think of a time when you saw danger coming to yourself or someone else. Use the key vocabulary to describe how you responded.

2. Although infectious diseases (those that spread from person to person) are still a very serious problem, the percentage of deaths from such diseases is far smaller than it was 200—or even 100—years ago. For example, in eighteenth-century Europe, about 400,000 people died each year of smallpox. By the late twentieth century, the disease had been virtually wiped out. (The last known case of someone catching it from another person occurred in 1977.)

    Write an essay in which you describe, in detail, one case (or a few related cases) in which a serious disease was brought under control by medical science in the past 200 years or so. Tell the story of the disease-control effort and describe in detail the methods by which effective control became possible.

    Use the key vocabulary from this chapter as much as possible in your essay.

3. Every society contains some people or organizations that are more powerful than others, and it's not difficult to find cases in which powerful people take advantage of less-powerful people. For example, rich and powerful people might be able to influence governments so that laws are written to favor them or their friends and perhaps to hurt people who are not powerful enough to influence the government in this way. For another example, the owner of an apartment building might try to save money by not doing necessary repairs and maintenance to the building. Even if some of the people who live in the building are hurt because of this failure to make necessary repairs, the powerful owner of the building might avoid punishment because he or she has enough money to pay for lawyers and the protection they provide.

    It has often been said that one of the jobs of government is to protect the weak from the powerful. Write an essay in which you describe some ways that powerful people or groups can or should be restricted by the law so that they cannot exploit less-powerful people. If possible, you should support your essay by showing real examples of exploitation by the powerful and by explaining how your solutions would have prevented this exploitation.

Use the key vocabulary from this chapter as much as possible in your essay.

4. Nearly every continent on Earth has undergone some recent desertification—the spreading of desert land into areas that used to be grassland or forest. The economic and social consequences of desertification can be very severe, as populations are forced to move from no-longer-useful lands (often to already overcrowded cities) and the agricultural production of formerly productive land drops to near zero. Also, barren land erodes more easily, experiences greater temperature extremes, and doesn't help recycle atmospheric CO_2. This problem has been especially serious in Africa, where (for example) the huge Sahara desert has been spreading into areas that used to be able to support farming and grazing. However, desertification has also been going on in such widely diverse areas as Australia, the southwestern U.S., Mexico, central Asia, Israel, Jordan, Brazil, and even Iceland. Many causes have been blamed for this phenomenon—including overpopulation, global climate change, bad farming practices, greedy or incompetent governments, and many others. Similarly, a lot of research has been done to suggest ways of stopping, or even reversing, desertification.

Write an essay in which you suggest the best way(s) to stop or slow down desertification. This is a very large and complex topic, so—to avoid being too general—you should limit your essay in such a way that its subject can be handled in the space you have. You might choose to limit your focus to one or a few countries or regions, to one or a few solutions, or to some other manageable subdivision of the topic.

Use the key vocabulary from this chapter as much as possible in your essay. (*Note:* You might also want to look at the vocabulary in chap. 7, "Causes and Effects" and chap. 8, "Permitting, Making Easier".)

Additional Vocabulary by Chapter

Chapter 1

access
accurate
advocate (v)
arthritis
autopsy
budget
cocktail
commute
compass
component
composite
county
currency
digital environment
massage
measure
meticulous
mystery
nuclear family
nucleus
offensive
opposition
protocol
reluctant
reproductive system
sexually explicit
shores
string quartet
superficial
tastes
therapy
time-consuming
trading

Chapter 2

appeal (v)
applicant
battle
bland
character
coating
contract (v)
culture
evidence
expand
illegible
loan
misfit
originate
poll
press
punitive
quarantine
regulator
short-list
spread
strict
survivor
target
tumor

Chapter 3

achieve
add to
admit (to a school)
create
defer to
design (n)

environmental
faculty
famine
flow
glacier
herb
large-scale
leader of the pack
natural resources
novel (n)
prohibition
reggae
robin
species
stationary
understated
virtually
wither
workplace

Chapter 4

attend to
auditor
boom
career
confiscate
distaste
disturbing
immoral
income
infrastructure
innocent
lack
massive

negotiator
obstacle
otherwise
parent company
portfolio
puzzling
regulation
respond
revenue
revolution
savvy
tornado

Chapter 5
advocate (n)
atmosphere
consensus
debt
dependence
dominated
eyesight
fatigue
feminist
financial
fossil fuels
fuel-efficient
genome
influence
leak
militant
prospective
run on (a fuel)
scandal
seal (n)
standard
veteran

Chapter 6
ache
adulthood
affluent
algae

bald
birthrate
cardiac
cello
chain
coincidence
depression
emphasize
fever
freckle
immigration
jet lag
lactase
millet
outbreak
pliers
population
suicide
time zone
two-ply
wage

Chapter 7
airflow
automate
bacterium
campaign
collapse (n)
colonialism
corruption
delay
deterioration
devaluation
flexible
funding
gang
infect
labor unrest
lax
licensed products
opaque
quality control

rampant
sacrifice (n)
senior
slash-and-burn
speechless
strike (n)

Chapter 8
cash flow
circulation
convicted
criticize
cut costs
deployment
enforce
evaporation
headache
interview
market economy
personal
raised
resignation
retirement
sentence
toll
transition
troops
upbringing
vents
victim

Chapter 9
amnesty
appeal (n)
aspirin
campus
chair (a person)
collapse (v)
drug trafficking
fine
get under way
imprison

indefinitely

injury

interest rate

mall

outcry

overdue

patrol

power outage

rage

swift

talented

tidal wave

vaccine

Alphabetical Listing of Additional Vocabulary

Numbers in parentheses indicate the chapters in which items are presented.

access (1)
accurate (1)
ache (6)
achieve (3)
add to (3)
admit (to a school) (3)
adulthood (6)
advocate (n) (5)
advocate (v) (1)
affluent (6)
airflow (7)
algae (6)
amnesty (9)
appeal (n) (9)
appeal (v) (2)
applicant (2)
arthritis (1)
aspirin (9)
atmosphere (5)
attend to (4)
auditor (4)
automate (7)
autopsy (1)

bacterium (7)
bald (6)
battle (2)
birthrate (6)
bland (2)
boom (4)
budget (1)

campaign (7)
campus (9)
cardiac (6)
career (4)
cash flow (8)
cello (6)
chain (6)
chair (a person) (9)
character (2)
circulation (8)
coating (2)
cocktail (1)
coincidence (6)
collapse (n) (7)
collapse (v) (9)
colonialism (7)
commute (1)
compass (1)
component (1)
composite (1)
confiscate (4)
consensus (5)
contract (v) (2)
convicted (8)
corruption (7)
county (1)
create (3)
criticize (8)
culture (2)
currency (1)
cut costs (8)

debt (5)
defer to (3)
delay (7)
dependence (5)
deployment (8)
depression (6)
design (n) (3)
deterioration (7)
devaluation (7)
digital environment (1)
distaste (4)
disturbing (4)
dominated (5)
drug trafficking (9)

emphasize (6)
enforce (8)
environmental (3)
evaporation (8)
evidence (2)
expand (2)
eyesight (5)

faculty (3)
famine (3)
fatigue (5)
feminist (5)
fever (6)
financial (5)
fine (9)
flexible (7)

flow (3)

fossil fuels (5)

freckle (6)

fuel-efficient (5)

funding (7)

gang (7)

genome (5)

get under way (9)

glacier (3)

headache (8)

herb (3)

illegible (2)

immigration (6)

immoral (4)

imprison (9)

income (4)

indefinitely (9)

infect (7)

influence (5)

infrastructure (4)

injury (9)

innocent (4)

interest rate (9)

interview (8)

jet lag (6)

labor unrest (7)

lack (4)

lactase (6)

large-scale (3)

lax (7)

leader of the pack (3)

leak (5)

licensed products (7)

loan (2)

mall (9)

market economy (8)

massage (1)

massive (4)

measure (1)

meticulous (1)

militant (5)

millet (6)

misfit (2)

mystery (1)

natural resources (3)

negotiator (4)

novel (n) (3)

nuclear family (1)

nucleus (1)

obstacle (4)

offensive (1)

opaque (7)

opposition (1)

originate (2)

otherwise (4)

outbreak (6)

outcry (9)

overdue (9)

parent company (4)

patrol (9)

personal (8)

pliers (6)

poll (2)

population (6)

portfolio (4)

power outage (9)

press (2)

prohibition (3)

prospective (5)

protocol (1)

punitive (2)

puzzling (4)

quality control (7)

quarantine (2)

rage (9)

raised (8)

rampant (7)

reggae (3)

regulation (4)

regulator (2)

reluctant (1)

reproductive system (1)

resignation (8)

respond (4)

retirement (8)

revenue (4)

revolution (4)

robin (3)

run on (a fuel) (5)

sacrifice (n) (7)

savvy (4)

scandal (5)

seal (n) (5)

senior (7)

sentence (8)

sexually explicit (1)

shores (1)

short-list (2)

slash-and-burn (7)

species (3)

speechless (7)

spread (2)

standard (5)

stationary (3)

strict (2)

strike (n) (7)

string quartet (1)

suicide (6)

superficial (1)

survivor (2)

swift (9)

talented (9)

target (2)

tastes (1)

therapy (1)

tidal wave (9)

time-consuming (1)

time zone (6)

toll (8)

tornado (4)

trading (1)

transition (8)

troops (8)

tumor (2)

two-ply (6)

understated (3)

upbringing (8)

vaccine (9)

vents (8)

veteran (5)

victim (8)

virtually (3)

wage (6)

wither (3)

workplace (3)

Answer Key

Abbreviations and Codes

Where the key lists two or more answers separated by commas, each listed answer is possible. If two or more answers are separated by a semicolon, the first answer is for the first blank in the question, the second answer is for the second blank, etc.

Brackets [ ] indicate an answer that is possible but slightly less acceptable than another answer

"various" = a wide variety of answers could be given

"e.g." = for example

". . ." = and so on, as in the original

Chapter 1. Including, Making Up

1.1. 1. involves 2. contains [includes] 3. consists of 4. composed 5. encompasses, comprises, [involves] 6. consists

1.2. various, e.g., 1. The economic stimulus package contains laws controlling interest rates, rules protecting . . . 2. A modern symphony orchestra consists of strings, brass, . . . 3. One group, composed of people over the age of 60, expressed strong opposition to building new schools. 4. Cleaning up an oil spill involves several difficult procedures, including trapping the spill in floating booms, cleaning the shore . . . 5. The fluid delivery system comprises a pump, a valve, . . .

1.3. 1. make up, constitute 2. form 3. All told 4. make up, constitute 5. Mainstream 6. comprehensive

1.4. various, e.g., 1. Children between the ages of 5 and 14 make up most of the movie audience on Saturday afternoons. 2. The university's review of its programs was comprehensive. 3. All told, there are four ways for our company to increase its sales. 4. Cable, fiber-optic phone lines, and wireless digital receivers constitute the group of high-speed Internet connections. 5. The mainstream American attitude toward government is that . . .

1.5. 1. c 2. f 3. b 4. g 5. e 6. d 7. a

1.6. 1. includes 2. form 3. comprehensive 4. contains 5. make up

1.7. 1. of 2. up 3. all 4. various, e.g., Becoming a doctor 5. various, e.g., A water molecule 6. various, e.g., society 7. various, e.g., the citrus fruits 8. various, e.g., string quartet 9. various, e.g., a range of techniques from

1.8. various

1.9. 1. c 2. g 3. f 4. k 5. h 6. j 7. d 8. 1 9. e 10. b 11. a 12. i

1.10. 1. accurate 2. superficial 3. reproductive system 4. commute 5. meticulously 6. arthritis 7. time-consuming 8. advocated 9. protocol 10. Autopsies

1.11. Answers will vary widely.

Chapter 2. Excluding, Not Being Part Of

2.1. 1. in that 2. various, e.g., sole 3. various, e.g., relief 4. various, e.g., behavior

2.2. various, e.g., 1. Sarah was socially marginal at the school because she dressed differently . . . 2. Venezuela and Mexico are anomalous among the members of OPEC because . . . 3. The government's egregious spending on projects that enriched the prime minister's friends made the public angry. 4. The Cuban pine is anomalous among pine trees in that . . .

2.3. 1. filter 2. screen 3. exclude

2.4. 1. out 2. through 3. various, e.g., them 4. on

2.5. various, e.g., 1. The high cost of tuition at Barstoke University kept most middle-class students out. 2. In hiring pilots, airlines use psychological tests to screen out unstable people. 3. The military authorities banned journalists from the battle zone. 4. The government, because it was anti-American, excluded American companies from the country. 5. High air pressure inside the building keeps out the dusty outside air.

2.6. 1. state, nation 2. to 3. social 4. from

2.7. various, e.g., 1. There is still no evidence that even microscopic alien life forms have ever come to Earth. 2. DeBoer liked to portray himself as a social outcast, but he was actually quite popular, and his paintings sold well during his lifetime. 3. The research showed that the cells were damaged by rogue proteins. 4. Many of the beliefs held by Western animal-rights activists seem alien to people from poorer, more rural societies.

2.8. 1. h 2. k 3. g 4. e 5. i 6. d 7. j 8. f 9. a 10. c 11. b

2.9. 1. screened 2. exception 3. marginally 4. filtered 5. ban 6. anomalous 7. exclude [filter out]

2.10. 1. trader 2. concept 3. social 4. imports 5. rule 6. behavior

2.11. 1. from items 2–8, various, e.g., 2. trader 3. they are birds but they can't fly 4. spending 5. make 6. airborne dirt 7. Mexico 8. a criminal record

2.12. 1. e 2. l 3. k 4. c 5. b 6. j 7. i 8. a 9. f 10. g 11. d 12. h

2.13. 1. strict 2. bland 3. short-listed 4. expands; contracts 5. evidence 6. survivors 7. originated; spread 8. appeal

2.14. Answers will vary widely.

Chapter 3. Equivalence, Similarity

3.1. 1. with 2. with 3. between 4. various, e.g., the property bubble in Japan 5. various, e.g., the music of the 1980s

3.2. various, e.g., 1. It would cost hundreds of thousands of dollars to create parity between our laboratory and those at other universities. 2. The Puritans left England for Holland after they realized they could never gain equality with other groups within the Church of England. 3. The religious art of western South America parallels that of some Pacific islands. 4. Some parts of the president's speech last night echoed statements made by John F. Kennedy in 1962. 5. Smithing metal parallels blowing glass in that both involve heating a substance until it can be shaped.

3.3. 1. parallel 2. echo 3. parity

3.4. 1. old 2. various, e.g., women suffer from gender discrimination 3. to 4. various, e.g., virtually 5. various, e.g., write a short passage

3.5. various, e.g., 1. Just as flat-screen displays make laptop computers possible, they make it possible to . . . 2. Mohandas Gandhi urged nonviolent resistance to injustice. Martin Luther King, Jr., did likewise. 3. The Great Plains of North America and the steppes of Asia are alike in that both are temperate-zone grasslands. 4. Even though some U.S. "silver dollars" are not actually made of silver, they are equivalent in face value to those that are pure silver. 5. Though very different, English and Hindi alike come from the ancient tongue known as Proto-Indo-European.

3.6. 1. various, e.g., Richard Nixon 2. in 3. of 4. in

3.7. various, e.g., 1. Robertson is just a clone of Mayor LaGuardia. 2. The Inland Revenue Authority is Singapore's counterpart of the Internal Revenue Service. 3. The streets of New Hartford were laid out in the image of those of Hartford, Connecticut. 4. The new X-IS computer is a clone of the Portway 2100 system. 5. Todd Wilson is in charge of quality control at Dobson Hydraulics. His counterpart at MNO Hydraulics is Marla Spreese.

3.8. 1. l 2. g 3. j 4. c 5. i 6. k 7. a 8. d 9. e 10. f 11. b 12. h

3.9. 1. parity [equality] 2. likewise 3. counterpart 4. echo 5. paralleled 6. equivalent

3.10. 1. various, e.g., achieved 2. in that 3. does 4. of 5.various, e.g., virtually 6. various, e.g., a famine 7. between

3.11. 1. h 2. b 3. d 4. j 5. g 6. l 7. f 8. a 9. i 10. c 11. k 12. e

3.12. 1. understated 2. stationary 3. workplace 4. species 5. add to 6. achieve 7. large-scale 8. admit 9. glacier 10. faculty 11. defer to 12. created

3.13. Answers will vary widely.

Chapter 4. Difference, Inequality

4.1. 1. from 2. correct 3. between; and 4. from; by 5. from 6. among

4.2. various, e.g., 1. The planets known as gas giants differ from the other planets in that they don't have actual surfaces. 2. After the company was split up, the marketing plans of the various divisions diverged. 3. There was a great disparity between what management promised its workers and what it actually delivered. 4. There is an inequality in access to government services, with the Govanese having far less than other citizens. 5. Because of the disparity between incomes in Africa and North America, African customers can't be expected to pay the same for a CD as North Americans do. 6. Traditionally, the race of the performer distinguished Cajun music from zydeco. 7. We need judges who can differentiate between truly dangerous criminals and basically good people who have simply made a mistake.

4.3. 1. various, e.g., collection 2. in 3. various, e.g., organizations 4. various, e.g., personal computers 5. various, e.g., ecosystem

4.4. various, e.g., 1. . . . when you look at it through a microscope, you can see discrete cells. 2. . . . to find common interests among the state's disparate ethnic groups. 3. Because the Onawanda School District was not ethnically very diverse, . . . 4. Professor Gardenia's shelves held a heterogeneous mixture of objects . . . 5. Many visitors are surprised by New Zealand's diverse ecosystems . . .

4.5. 1. between 2. various, e.g., clear 3. bridge, close 4. various, e.g., created

4.6. various, e.g., 1. At Fastridge High School, there's a big contrast between the life of an athlete (who is likely to get a lot of attention) and that of a nonathlete. 2. At Fukuichi Systems, the contrast is obvious between the expensive cars at the executive parking area and the junkers at other areas of the lot. 3. The discrepancy between Livia's account and those of her friends is pretty large. She says she got home by 10:30, but they say she was at the club until at least midnight. 4. There's a big gap between our expectations and reality, in that we had expected a profit after about 18 months but are still posting losses.

4.7. 1. i 2. h 3. g 4. b 5. e 6. a 7. c 8. d 9. f 10. j
4.8. 1. diverge 2. discrepancy 3. disparity 4. distinguished 5. differ 6. discrete
4.9. 1. diverse [heterogeneous] 2. diverge 3. diverse 4. differentiates
      5. distinguishing 6. gap 7. discrete 8. differ 9. inequality 10. disparate
4.10. 1. by 2. in 3. various, e.g., Top-quality research 4. various, e.g., breaking
      5. various, e.g., immigration 6. various, e.g., good TV; bad TV 7. various, e.g.,
      My tastes in music 8. various, e.g., their attitudes toward government 9. various,
      e.g., the attitudes of labor; those of management 10. rich countries and poor
      countries
4.11. 1. f 2. i 3. b 4. j 5. l 6. c 7. h 8. k 9. d 10. g 11. a 12. e
4.12. 1. immoral 2. parent company 3. income 4. boom 5. Otherwise 6. revolutions
      7. innocent 8. puzzling 9. auditor 10. obstacle
4.13. Answers will vary widely.

Chapter 5. Changes, Increases, Decreases

5.1. 1. in, [to] 2. from; to 3. in, to 4. to
5.2. various, e.g., 1. Cotton farming has radically altered the size of the Aral Sea in
      Kazakhstan by . . . 2. Some European economies are in transition from a socialist
      system to a free-market system. 3. Some analysts say that birth-control pills . . .
      helped alter the role of women in American society. 4. After Hong Kong became
      . . . GlobeVest Telecommunications, Inc., had to modify its marketing
      plan. 5. Over the years, North American beliefs have altered so that it is now com-
      mon for people to consider environmental preservation more important than eco-
      nomic growth.
5.3. a. restructure b. transform c. restructure; redesign
5.4. 1. various, e.g., underwent 2. from; into 3. various, e.g., stock exchanges 4. debt
5.5. various, e.g., 1. It was clear that Hanscomb would have to redesign its CD players,
      which worked well but looked old fashioned. 2. The consultant recommended that
      Growtech, Inc., restructure to give employees more room to act on their creative
      ideas. 3. A government that wants to increase productivity by encouraging "creative
      thinking" has to transform an entire social system. . . . 4. Years of chaos . . . have
      transformed Abaca from a well-organized place with a good infrastructure into a
      desperately disorganized, primitive place. 5. Our system of frequent elections has
      to be redesigned so that congresspersons can concentrate on their jobs instead of
      worrying about being reelected.
5.6. 1. by 2. pay 3. various, e.g., sales force 4. various, e.g., pace
5.7. various, e.g., 1. . . . the use of the Greek language expanded far beyond what we
      normally think of as the Greek islands. 2. . . . the spread of tuberculosis through
      Europe and North America accelerated. 3. . . . sea level rises. 4. . . . and this raised
      Costa Rica's standard of living to near the top in the region.
5.8. 1. various, e.g., because 2. various, e.g., greatly 3. expand 4. various, e.g., the
      price 5. in 6. in
5.9. various, e.g., 1. . . . forced them to greatly reduce their estimates. 2. . . . and
      argued for reducing the benefits given out through this system. 3. . . . The natural
      beauty of the region declined as forests were choked and marshes were poisoned.
      4. . . . the quality of his writing and his influence among New York publishers both
      diminished. 5. . . . the market for coal contracted.
5.10. 1. g 2. k 3. i 4. f 5. m 6. d 7. l 8. e 9. n 10. a 11. j 12. c 13. b 14. h
5.11. 1. accelerate 2. expand 3. redesign 4. transition 5. contracts 6. modify

5.12. 1. redesign 2. declined [diminished] 3. restructuring 4. expand 5. rise
6. transformation; reduced 7. rose 8. in transition 9. altering

5.13. 1. to 2. various, e.g., underwent 3. various, e.g., soil 4. by 5. various, e.g.,
organizations 6. various, e.g., overseas sale of U.S. television programs 7. various,
e.g., Competition with the Soviet Union 8. various, e.g., violence on school
property 9. various, e.g., in ground temperature 10. various, e.g., making; to

5.14. 1. f 2. d 3. g 4. e 5. j 6. b 7. a 8. 1 9. c 10. k 11. h 12. i

5.15. 1. dominated 2. leak 3. scandals 4. advocates 5. dependence 6. influence;
consensus 7. run on 8. veterans

5.16. Answers will vary widely.

Chapter 6. Links, Correlations, Happening Together

6.1. 1. between 2. with 3. various, e.g., Air and water pollution 4. various, e.g.,
monsoon rains

6.2. various, e.g., 1. A tendency to vote for liberal candidates often goes along with
vegetarianism. 2. A recent survey showed a high correlation between health club
membership and an income greater than $50,000. 3. Outbreaks of diseases often
accompany social unrest, such as civil wars or revolutions. 4. A harvest festival of
some kind is likely to accompany an agricultural tradition in society. 5. Lower-
than-normal levels of testosterone have been linked to a feeling of sudden weakness
in a man's arms and legs.

6.3. 1. is 2. that are 3. various, e.g., it will regulate potentially dangerous industries
4. various, e.g., have electronic crowd-control systems 5. various, e.g., The decline
of downtown businesses

6.4. various, e.g., 1. Frequent small earthquakes are often associated with natural hot
springs or geysers. 2. Workers are likely to be loyal to their employers to the
degree that the workers are given control over planning their own time. 3. A very
short lifespan and very small size are characteristic of animals that reproduce
frequently and copiously. 4. A bachelor's degree (or higher) is characteristic of the
public-broadcasting audience. 5. In the Great Lakes region, Indian burial mounds
are strongly associated with the finding of old arrowheads and pieces of pottery.

6.5. 1. imply 2. infer 3. imply

6.6. 1. that 2. from 3. various, e.g., that the protesters were well organized 4. various,
e.g., that the victim had been murdered

6.7. various, e.g., 1. Because the article was published in the most important British
journal of science, most readers inferred that it was reliable. 2. Montego fever
implied high levels of sybillomasine in the blood. 3. In a satellite photograph, an
area of high, wavy clouds implies strong upper-level winds. 4. When I walked into
the meeting, I inferred from people's faces that I was in serious trouble.

6.8. 1. d 2. h 3. b 4. i 5. g 6. j 7. f 8. c 9. a 10. e

6.9. various, e.g., 1. If you chose Halloween, you might say, "pumpkins, costumes,
ghosts . . ." 2. jet lag, fatigue, disorientation 3. low unemployment, a rising stock
market, public confidence 4. energy, an eagerness to go to work, good relations
with your co-workers 5. graying hair, wrinkling of the skin, greater patience in
hard times

6.10. 1. link 2. associated 3. infer 4. imply 5. accompanied

6.11. 1. correlation 2. associated 3. implies 4. associated with 5. to the degree
that 6. link between

6.12. 1. to 2. occur 3. strong 4. various, e.g.,The police 5. various, e.g., adolescence 6. various, e.g., taking their product; the development of cancer 7. various, e.g., a lack of self-confidence 8. various, e.g., a government loses touch with its people 9. various, e.g., A slow-running drain 10. various, e.g., the number of its moons

6.13. various, e.g., 1. Skill in playing basketball is often linked to a person's height. 2. A desire to dress differently from one's parents goes along with becoming a teenager. 3. A feeling of tiredness often accompanies low levels of blood sugar. 4. Freckles are often associated with red hair. 5. Security checks at the airport were increased in conjunction with the pope's visit. 6. Extremely high levels of cholesterol in the blood imply a poor diet. 7. Marital trouble often develops in correlation with unhappiness in one's job. 8. A highly mobile population is characteristic of societies that place a high value on job success. 9. To the degree that a country's government is corrupt, foreign companies will be reluctant to invest there. 10. We can infer from the rising popularity of Asian medicines that there will be an increased threat to the populations of such animals as the sun bear and the rhinoceros.

6.14. 1. e 2. f 3. i 4. k 5. n 6. m 7. o 8. c 9. b 10. a 11. l 12. g 13. j 14. d 15. h

6.15. 1. freckles 2. algae 3. cello 4. jet lag 5. population 6. bald 7. depression 8. two-ply 9. suicide 10. coincidence

6.16. Answers will vary widely.

Chapter 7. Causes and Effects

7.1. 1. stems from, derives from 2. yielded, generated 3. was; due to 4. is generated by, derives from, [is due to] 5. generated 6. led to

7.2. various, e.g., 1. Hard times for the makers of vinyl record albums stemmed from a public demand for compact discs. 2. Careful attention to detail in the experiment yielded highly reliable findings. 3. If someone feels ill after drinking milk, the problem is probably due to a difficulty in digesting milk, not to an allergy. 4. Latin's importance in all fields of study during the Renaissance derived from its association with the still-powerful Catholic Church. 5. Increasing the amount of sugar in the mixture causes the yeast to generate more carbon dioxide. 6. The hiring of more part-time workers led to great anxiety among the university's full-time staff.

7.3. various, e.g., 1. sick 2. changes 3. a better relationship 4. unemployable

7.4. various, e.g., 1. Researchers found that a lack of decision-making power rendered workers less efficient. 2. Strong upper-level winds and high humidity favor the formation of tornadoes. 3. Small, windowless rooms make some people anxious and fearful. 4. Easy access to iron and coal promoted the development of a steel industry near the Great Lakes. 5. Current conditions in the eastern Caribbean Sea favor the formation of hurricanes.

7.5. 1. for 2. on 3. various, e.g., open warfare 4. for 5. for

7.6. various, e.g., 1. High winds were responsible for the rapid spread of the grass fires. 2. At one time, evil spirits were blamed for what we now call mental illness. 3. A great pressure buildup behind the front panel was responsible for its warping. 4. The investigators said that pilot error was responsible for the crash. 5. The students loudly denied breaking the window after they were blamed for it by the teacher. 6. The children's failure to return home before dark provoked great concern among the parents.

7.7. 1. i 2. l 3. b 4. h 5. g 6. f 7. m 8. d 9. k 10. j 11. c 12. e 13. a. *Note:* Although number 11 could match either "a" or "c," only "a" can go with number 13, so "c" is a better answer for 11.

7.8. 1. provoked 2. generated 3. make 4. was responsible for 5. promote; yield 6. leads to

7.9. various, e.g., 1. jump 2. The lack of government regulation in the television industry 3. the growth of mold 4. fear in neighboring countries 5. the shipping accident 6. great excitement in the crowd 7. difficult to pass 8. a steam explosion 9. The fallout of ash in Singapore and Malaysia 10. serious flooding

7.10. 1. j 2. k 3. h 4. f 5. l 6. b 7. d 8. e 9. c 10. g 11. a 12. i

7.11. 1. bacterium 2. colonialism 3. devalue 4. collapsed 5. automate 6. flexible 7. campaign 8. rampant 9. airflow 10. Labor unrest

7.12. Answers will vary widely.

Chapter 8. Permitting, Making Easier

8.1. 1. lenient 2. permissive 3. permit 4. lenient

8.2. 1. with 2. to 3. shown; toward 4. various, e.g., parents 5. various, e.g., grants 6. various, e.g., businesses to do socially irresponsible things

8.3. various, e.g., 1. Improving our cash flow would allow us to buy some new computers. 2. The store's permissiveness with its employees gives the company a bad image. 3. If you want to use a company car, you'll need your supervisor's permission. 4. We can allow students to make a few small changes in their research proposals. 5. Illegal photocopying continues because the courts have been so lenient with wrongdoers. 6. The program will not allow any character other than a letter or a number in a password. 7. Loose and sandy soil allows good rainwater drainage.

8.4. 1. exempt 2. excuse 3. consent 4. approval

8.5. 1. gave; to 2. from 3. for 4. from 5. to

8.6. various, e.g., 1. Any professional photographer knows that you can't publish a photograph without the written consent of the people who appear in it. 2. Very small businesses—those with fewer than 10 employees—are exempt from the government's racial-diversity guidelines. 3. Our proposal to redesign the company's logo failed because we couldn't get approval from the marketing manager. 4. The medical procedure was dangerous, but Mr. Harkins gave the doctors his consent.

8.7. various, e.g., 1. the decision process 2. Governor Smith's entry 3. Some new data 4. peace 5. Approval by the Security Council

8.8. various, e.g., 1. Draining the swamp facilitated the entry of sugar farming into the area. 2. The Harpers' divorce removed a major obstacle to their seeing the people they truly loved. 3. Increased funding eased the police efforts to enforce laws against drunk driving. 4. An exemption from the English language test cleared the way for Andreas to take a full load of English classes. 5. I don't want to take sides in this argument, but I'm willing to facilitate a settlement.

8.9. 1. g 2. k 3. b 4. e 5. f 6. j 7. i 8. c 9. a 10. d 11. h

8.10. 1. allow 2. lenient 3. facilitate 4. exempt 5. excused, [exempt] 6. approval 7. consenting

8.11. various, e.g., 1. transition 2. with; sales have declined 3. gave; a tour 4. taxis 5. us to access the Internet 6. The new law 7. employees to make personal phone calls

8.12. 1. f 2. i 3. k 4. h 5. e 6. j 7. b 8. c 9. d 10. a 11. h

8.13. 1. cutting costs 2. interviews 3. vent 4. headache 5. criticized 6. convicted
7. deploy 8. sentencing
8.14. Answers will vary widely.

Chapter 9. Stopping, Preventing
9.1. 1. various, e.g., ground 2. for 3. various, e.g., looking 4. various, e.g., New
regulations 5. various, e.g., amaze me
9.2. various, e.g., 1. A court order halted the company's sales of the insecticide known
as Fortidonic because it had been connected to serious illnesses in humans. 2. In
the condition known as Herberger's disease, the pituitary gland ceases the production of hormones necessary for the normal development of the human body. 3. Relations between the two companies became so bad that they ceased sharing information with one another about new developments in the market. 4. The Delaney
family suspended their donations to St. Aikman's College because they disliked the
college's president.
9.3. 1. myself 2. to 3. various, e.g., them 4. various, e.g., to park on campus 5. various,
e.g., the expression of antigovernment opinions
9.4. various, e.g., 1. The law forbids a judge to be in charge of any case involving a
company in which he or she owns shares. 2. After Mr. Harcourt was arrested, the
police denied him the use of a telephone to call his lawyer. 3. Most people who
tour the White House are restricted to certain public or ceremonial rooms. . . .
4. . . . Any employee who wants to develop a romantic relationship with another
should restrain him- or herself.
9.5. 1. in 2. from 3. various, e.g., obesity 4. various, e.g., him from taking any action
5. various, e.g., the pain
9.6. various, e.g., 1. Troops loyal to the government blocked an attempted coup by
General Fletcher. 2. A lack of training in statistics hinders many managers in their
jobs. 3. Researchers found that mixing large amounts of sunflower oil into rats'
food forestalled some signs of aging, such as wrinkled skin and a loss of muscle
mass. 4. Some people think the death penalty deters such serious crimes as murder
and rape. 5. A televised emotional appeal from the mother of one of the hostages
prevented the kidnappers from killing their hostages.
9.7. 1. k 2. a 3. l 4. g 5. b 6. j 7. h 8. d 9. f 10. c 11. i 12. e
9.8. various, e.g., 1. movement, access, etc. 2. employment, research, etc. 3. death,
aging, etc.
9.9. 1. cease 2. denied 3. restraint 4. block 5. prevent 6. restricted
9.10. 1. forbids 2. forestall 3. prevent 4. restricted 5. suspended 6. ceased 7. restrain
8. blocking 9. denied 10. halt
9.11. 1. desist 2. until 3. various, e.g., shout 4. from 5. various, e.g., forest fires
6. various, e.g., to their training area 7. various, e.g., to enter the convention
center; their entry 8. various, e.g., an outbreak of fighting 9. him or her many
jobs
9.12. 1. l 2. f 3. b 4. g 5. j 6. d 7. k 8. a 9. c 10. i 11. h 12. e
9.13. 1. drug trafficking 2. aspirin 3. interest rate 4. got under way 5. collapse
6. talented 7. patrol 8. power outage 9. appeal 10. rage
9.14. Answers will vary widely.